Awakening the Goddess

33 Sacred Practices for Healing, Self-Love
& Embodying the Divine Feminine

By: Krystal Aranyani

This book is dedicated to my Mother Darlene,
To Mahadevi, the Great Goddess.
To the Goddesses who showed us the way,
And to the Goddesses to follow our path.

✧

I also dedicate this to Vishuddha Das, my Beloved,
And to all the Gods who have the courage to
Rise up and stand tall with Goddesses.
May we find our way back home, as One.

Sat Nam.

Table of Contents

Note to the Reader

It took me twenty-five years to sit in front of a mirror, look myself in the eyes and say, "I love you," and truly mean it. We have been raised in a society that highly profits from our feelings of inadequacy. Guilt, doubt, loneliness, separation, feelings of not being enough or of being too much have become our collective consciousness. It's time we rise above and embrace our epic essence! We will no longer play small, hiding our light and neglecting our divine nature in order to make others comfortable or as a result of what society has taught us.

We are all divine beings of light. That's right—you ARE divine. Yes, you. You are perfect just the way you are. Right here, right now. You are a living, dazzling child of the cosmos, dancing through time and space as a precious expression of Goddess and God. This book is written not to teach you anything new, but only to remind you of what is already within. Your DNA is encoded with this sacred knowledge, I'm just here to help guide you along the path of rediscovering and reclaiming your sovereignty.

Your divine light that illuminates your being is your personal power. You are not separate from the Divine, you never have been and it was only an illusion that led you to believe so. You may have spent many lifetimes believing so, but now is your remembrance. This journey back home is one of deep self-discovery, self-love, and self-awakening. While there are a couple of exercises in this book specifically for women, it is meant for everyone; we each have the Divine Feminine (and Masculine) within, which extends far beyond gender.

Because you are a wonder of the cosmos, a child of the Great Mother, you should love yourself. You really should. We are made of stars and are as big and important as the galaxies, the trees, and the oceans. We deserve to shine. Actually, we are MEANT to shine! It is our birthright. We are welcoming a new age of the Divine Feminine. Women are coming into their own power, rediscovering their voices, rising tall and shining brighter than ever before! Men are embracing their femininity, expressing their emotions openly when they used to be shamed for doing so, and taking on roles that once were only seen as the roles of women. The old way isn't working for us, nothing has been clearer. It's our conscious choice to now be part of this global awakening. It is time for us to step fearlessly into our personal power, embrace the sensual world before us and to stop shaming and hiding our Truth. It is time to liberate ourselves from past limiting beliefs and all that was once holding us back. It is important to note that this is not about overpowering the Divine Masculine, but instead it is about raising our Shakti to meet Shiva as One. This book is my offering to you, sisters and brothers, Goddesses and Gods, in it you will find an accumulation of everything I have practiced and blossomed from on my own self-love journey. I hope this knowledge will serve you as it has served me.

From one Goddess to another:
You are seen,
You are heard,
You are loved deeply.
We are in this together.

"I do not wish them [women] to have power over men; but over themselves." ~ *Mary Wollstonecraft*

My Story

It only seems right to begin a book about self-love with the story of my own self-love journey. Did I always love myself? And if not, how did I end up where I am today, writing this book for you?

When we are young, we love ourselves—we love everyone! That is, until society teaches us otherwise. As most young girls in today's western society (and most other societies for that matter), I grew up disconnected from my body not knowing what self-love meant. What I did know all about was self-hate. Once I hit puberty and started to become a woman, I—with zero guidance—went out into the world with stars in my eyes. Those stars were quickly replaced with green, jealousy, and red, hatred for myself. I was jealous of other girls, everything became a competition. I hated myself, why couldn't I be better? Why couldn't I be prettier? Smarter? Taller? Funnier? More popular?

I carried these thoughts with me from early puberty into my twenties. These years were filled with the struggles that come along with self-doubt, low self-esteem and self-worth, materialism, consumerism, alcoholism, anorexia, bulimia, binge eating, self-harming, toxic friendships, abusive partners, unhealthy sexual activities, and the constant feelings of not being enough. I was trying to find my worth in things that could never last. "I'll be whole as long as he never leaves me." "I'll like myself when I lose those last five pounds." "I'll be happy once I buy that dress." "I NEED that dress now or I cannot go on." For a moment I would be happy, but then I'd realize that it wasn't going to last so I would numb myself from reality. I remember nights staying awake wishing I could crawl out of my own skin and be someone new, someone different, anyone else but me. I wasn't just disconnected from my divine temple, I hated it. Inside and out. And I constantly let it know by the way I treated it.

I never learned the concept of respecting my body, sharing my mind or being proud of my soul. Everything that made me a woman seemed to either be shamed or sexualized in society. My first menstruation wasn't a time of sacredness but rather one of the most embarrassing days of my young life. After bleeding all over the boy I had a crush on's chair in front of my whole seventh grade class, the teacher quickly wrapped a sweater around my waist and gave me the day off school. "I'm so sorry this happened to you," she told me. I quickly learned that this was something to be hidden and ashamed of, as I was teased by my peers the following weeks afterwards. I started having sex at fifteen. My first time was special and with a boy I had been dating for a year, so I got lucky there. Every time I would get my period I would hide it and apologize to him profusely, like I had somehow wronged him. After we broke up and I experienced my first heartbreak, I filled that void with temporary lovers who didn't appreciate the act of sharing ourselves together, and so I began that search for finding my worth and seeking validation in things and people that would never last.

After the whirlwind of chaos and emotional turmoil that were my teenage years, I landed myself in several highly abusive relationships. These relationships were based upon dependence and needy attachment on my end, and neglect and lies on their end. I was able to ignore how I felt about my own self when I put all of my energy into someone else. As long as he was around and making me feel good I could survive, but the second he put me down or fed my fear of abandonment, I couldn't possibly go on. A funny thing with our human minds is that we tend to subconsciously choose partners who feed our worst fears, leaving us constantly on edge, rather than those who help them go away. As most abusive relationships go, I was on top of the world at the highest of highs, then like a rollercoaster dropping with no warning, my world suddenly came crashing before my eyes. Sometimes the break between would be a week, sometimes a day, other times an hour. This would often find me laying on the washroom floor for hours screaming in excruciating pain, praying for my life to end so my misery could be no more. This would go on daily for months on end. Somehow I became addicted to that rollercoaster and couldn't get off of it no matter how hard I tried. I clung on so tight that any relationship I was in would inevitably lead to suffering. I wanted to be loved so badly by everyone but myself.

When we would argue, I was told by these partners that I was only good to use as arm candy and for sex; I had no other positive attributes. Once you hear something enough you begin to believe it, and the only thing that had gotten me a significant amount of attention before that was my appearance and sexuality. One partner would often scream, "God only put you on this planet to wrap your legs around a pole!" whenever he would arrive home drunk to me sitting on the floor a crying, worried mess. I'm not sure if he was the one to plant the seed or if I would have ended up down the road of the sex industry on my own, but by my early twenties that's where I found myself, on the other side of the world with my legs wrapped around a pole. Perhaps I believed at the time that I couldn't be anything more and that was my ticket out of the life I was leading. Or maybe it was the fact that I had so much sexual energy flowing through me and the only way I knew how to appropriately deal with it was to secretly let it all loose while hiding that life from friends, family, and the rest of "normal" society. While I was in the industry, the men I was surrounded by continued to tell me that's all I was worth, and I believed them. I can't say where my self-love was at that point in my life, but going by the way I let them speak to me, it's apparent it was utterly non-existent.

I also can't say that I had some major epiphany one day and decided to start loving myself. No, it was a process, a true journey into myself, and it still is. A journey of gaining and losing. Of opening and surrendering. Of letting go and accepting. Of fighting and giving up. Again and again. Through all those painful years, there was always a strong feeling that I was meant for more, an innate knowing, even when everyone had always told me otherwise. I knew I would help heal others one day, it was just figuring out how to get there that was the problem. I had to help myself first. And I did, over the course of a decade. I washed away all of the societal conditioning, the lies I had been told about what happiness is, the ego that attached to everything and everyone, the media that taught me how I should look and behave, the scared little girl who couldn't understand why she was so unwanted, the memories of past lives where I was killed for having a voice, and finally the beliefs that were engrained in me by religions that were pushed upon me as a child. That "good girls don't do that", that I would be punished for my sins, that I should be ashamed of my sexuality, that all things divine are masculine.

My true self-love journey started when I began a new life for myself alone in Thailand, after the worldwide dancing and all the trauma from back home in Canada. I moved 5000 miles away from my old life because I kept going back full circle. I had to first discover what the secret to true happiness was. If it wasn't being skinny, driving a shiny new Carrera 911, and having a rich, handsome, semi-abusive husband, what could it be? The first step was spending time by myself and getting to know who I was. That was by far the most painful part, but I knew I couldn't continue numbing myself any longer. Once I sobered up long enough I realized I wasn't only numbing the bad, but also the good. That's not how I wanted to live my life. I wanted to experience true joy, even if it meant going through the bitter darkness to find it.

I began opening up, accepting my past and my shadow while letting go of the shame and guilt that had become part of daily life. I slowly shed off all the self-limiting and self-destructive layers until finally the beautiful, unique, and radiant being within was exposed. I later immersed myself in different cultures, studying numerous religions and ancient belief systems. I kept my mind open to all, eager to absorb anything anyone was willing to teach me about their background and beliefs. Eventually I realized that they all came back to the same thing. The Divine is within each of us and is accessible to every one of us if we only have the patience and commitment to discover it. And that is where true happiness lays, nowhere outside, but in our own Divine essence.

While exploring the outer world, Earth, I deeply explored the inner realms, consciousness. I tried every type of alternative healing you could imagine. I searched for and sought out secret women's ceremonies and rituals all around the globe. I danced naked on beaches with Australian Goddesses, went on deep drum journeys with African Goddesses, prayed with Thai Goddesses, sang under the moonlight with Malay Goddesses, cried my eyes out with Mexican Goddesses, meditated with Balinese Goddesses, smoked life-changing plants with Brazilian Goddesses, found myself reflected in the eyes of Chinese Goddesses, lived in a traveling bus with wild French Goddesses, celebrated my moon cycle with Nepali Goddesses, reconnected with Spirit in the desert alongside Emirati Goddesses, washed away my pain in glacier waters with Native American Goddesses, learned the power of movement with Cuban Goddesses, and opened my heart charka, after years of being closed, with healing Indian Goddesses. I discovered my inner power, my sacred womb space, and my limitless gifts as a woman in their presence. And although words can't express how grateful I am for these adventures and all the extraordinary Goddesses I have been ever so blessed to connect with, the real revelations, the true shedding of my outdated, toxic skins, was through the inner work I performed alone.

At one point, my adventures and hunger for truth brought me to the middle of a deep psychedelic journey led by a shaman in the outback of Australia. I didn't know anyone else there and had traveled across the country to take part in this gathering, after a colourful boy on a festival dance floor mentioned it to me. I knew in that moment that I had to find it and go, even if it were mostly to feed my curiosity. What I was really hoping for was some form of supreme realization, something that would change my life, and I was open to anything the universe had for me.

We were in a small hut as the sun was setting and I could feel the cold creeping in. Animals howled and sang in the distance as I was slowly coming back into my body after what felt like years floating far away from it, exploring the cosmos and eternal interconnectedness of consciousness. I could hear the shaman chanting over someone on the other side of the hut when he went silent, then his footsteps came straight towards me. He gently put both hands over my heart and I immediately felt us become One, there were no secrets between him and I, for I was him and he was I. We stayed there together for what felt like a century but maybe it was only a minute, breathing and sharing as one. Eventually, we opened our eyes at the same moment and looked into each other's perfectly reflected faces. He said in broken English, "You have very much to share. You have very much to say. Too much in there (he pointed to my heart). You must say, to all! What is stopping you? Get it out!" It was final. I knew I had to begin telling my story, even though finding and sharing my voice was the most terrifying thing I could ever do. I couldn't be quiet any longer.

And so I did, I began sharing my story while traveling, first in women's shelters then to anyone I believed it could help to hear. Through this I healed myself and rediscovered my voice while helping others along their own healing journeys. The importance of sharing our story is so profound at this time of global awakening because it is a way to reconnect and begin to grow together. All of the tragedies of the Earth right now are due to our separation. We used to be in tight-knit communities, in supportive and loving tribes. Let's make our way back there together. Looking back on my path, I now know everything played out in perfect, divine time and order. As I shared my story and began teaching yoga, I was finally embodying the woman I had always wanted to become, and it was time I fully embodied the Goddess. My path led me to Hinduism and Tantra. When I finally discovered the Goddesses, it was like every single cell in my body screamed: "YES!" Something came alive in me that I never knew before. Every one of the faces of Shakti resonated so deeply within me as I began to see myself as each and understand why I did the things I did. I began to understand who I truly was as a woman! All those years I spent hiding from myself, how could I expect to be happy or for anyone else to add to my happiness when I didn't know who I was or what made me scream YES!?

"YES!"

I AM powerful. I AM sensual. I AM sexual. I AM the Creatrix of all. I AM Divine. I AM woman. The Goddess is not outside of me but within, we are one and the same. We always have been.

In the following pages, you will find the rituals, meditations, and practices that I personally used to awaken the Goddess within, heal from my past, and fall madly in love with my-Self. Most of these don't cost anything, they just require an open mind, eager heart, and a hopeful soul.

PART ONE

Reclaiming the Goddess

"You are magnificent beyond measure, perfect in your imperfections and wonderfully made." ~ Abiola Abrams

Mirror Gazing

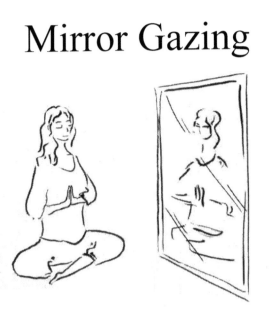

To fall in love with one's Self, we must first become comfortable with our Self. In our busy day to day lives of playing out so many roles (friend, mother, sister, coworker, partner), we often forget to stop for a few moments and appreciate everything it is that we do. We can't serve others to our fullest potential from an empty vessel. We must fill ourselves with self-acknowledgement, appreciation, and love before we can expect to send the same out into the world. During your self-love journey it is a must that you prioritize special time alone for growth, reflection, and revitalization. This isn't selfish, but it is necessary for your own personal evolution and the good of all. Once we love ourselves, we can then fully open our hearts to give and receive love unconditionally from others.

I will warn you, although this exercise may sound simple, it can play a significant part in your sacred journey. Proceed with gentle care.

What you will need: A mirror and your beautiful Self
Amount of Time: 11 minutes or longer

Note: It is recommended that you perform this for a minimum of forty days straight. If or when you feel ready, complete this exercise naked.

1. Sit tall in front of the mirror. Avoid slouching.

2. Close the eyes and take a few deep breaths, eight counts in, eight counts out, until you feel relaxed.

3. Open the eyes and stare deeply into their reflection.

4. Bring your palms together at heart centre

5. Tell yourself, "You are beautiful. You are Divine. I love you."

6. Bow to your reflection, honouring all that you are.

7. Look into your eyes again. Stay here for a few minutes, however long feels comfortable.

8. While staring into your eyes, begin to talk to yourself either aloud or silently, about how proud you are of your accomplishments. List these accomplishments.

9. Recognize any struggle you have been through that helped guide you to where you are today. To who you are today. Be proud.

10. Honour that you are here to witness all parts of yourself, the brilliant light a and the truthful darkness.

11. Acknowledge that you are opening yourself to personal growth and love in new forms. That takes courage.

12. Remind yourself that you are much more than this physical body, you are a divine being of infinite light and love.

13. When you feel you are done bring the palms back together and again bow to yourself.

14. Repeat: "You are beautiful. You are Divine. I love you." Relax here for a moment and take in your experience. Write it down if you'd like.

Divine Affirmations

Simply put, affirmations are statements that are spoken or written, and often repeated, to encourage, empower, and uplift the individual using them. What we think we become. Our reality is a direct product of our thoughts, so let's make them full of love, light, and divinity! Not only do our thoughts have the power to manifest into our physical reality, but they also each carry their own unique vibration. By simply surrounding yourself with positive words, you are already changing the vibration of your day and therefore your life. We've all heard of the law of attraction, right? Put what you would like to welcome into your life everywhere you can see, constantly reminding yourself of it. Get on the same vibration, and it shall appear. We literally have the power to create our reality. How glorious is that?

I should also mention that during the process of replacing your thoughts with more positive ones, don't be too hard on yourself when you have thoughts that can be perceived as negative. Try not to see this as a bad thing or judge yourself for them. They'll always be there at times, just remain open and receptive to the thoughts and reminders that set you on the path for success.

1. Firstly, ask yourself what you wish to attract in your life. Perhaps it is abundance, self-love, confidence, a new job or a new love. I suggest meditating on this for 5-10 minutes.

2. Now choose your affirmations and write them down on paper, speaking them aloud as you write. These are direct and present statements. Rather than saying "I want to attract my soulmate" say "I am attracting my soulmate now." Instead of saying "I want to love myself more" say "I love myself deeply". They should also not include any negative words. Rather than writing "Don't cry" try "I am calm".

3. If they don't come up for you right away or you have a problem putting them into a few words, just write out in full sentences everything you wish to attract into your life and how you are currently feeling. Look over the paper afterwards and circle any major or reoccurring words. Use one or two words each in a short sentence for one affirmation.

4. Keep your affirmations on a paper or notepad next to your bed to read every morning upon waking so you begin your day in a positive frame of mind. Put them on post-its where you'll see them often in the house, car or work. Set a notification on your phone to remind you throughout the day.

Examples of divine affirmations:

I am beautiful.

I am divine.

I am love.

I am enough.

I am whole.

I can and I will.

I radiate success.

I set my own limits.

I embody the Goddess.

My presence is my power.

I am manifesting abundance.

Others find me sexy and desirable.

I feel safe and comfortable in my body.

I see the divine within myself and all others.

I am in charge of how I feel and today I choose happiness.

I deserve the best and I accept only the best now.

It's my time. I am coming into my greatness.

I am choosing and not waiting to be chosen.

I overcome fears by following my dreams.

I am attracting the partner of my dreams.

I let go of all that no longer serves me.

My body is healthy and full of energy.

I will not compare myself to others.

I have the power to create change.

I am my own superhero.

When you're searching for ways to love yourself,
looking within is a great place to start.

Write it Out

How well do you really know yourself? Do you know exactly what makes you tick? Or what really makes you ticked off? Journaling can be one of the fastest ways to discovering your true Self. We sometimes get so caught up in relationships outside of ourselves, worrying about what others want and need, that we never figure out what we ourselves want and need. When I was younger, I was in a string of toxic relationships where I put all of my energy into my partners and friendships and didn't have my needs met in return. I was constantly filling up others' cups while mine remained almost completely emptied.

After years of going from one relationship to the next, I finally took the time to prioritize myself and discover who I was. To my surprise, I didn't know anything about myself! I had been disconnected and distracted from this wonderful, unique, and complex woman within my whole life! How can we expect others to understand us if we don't first understand ourselves? We must have a clear vision of who we are in order to get where and what we want from this life. Once I had a clearer understanding of who I was, I then respected myself enough to let go of the relationships and lifestyle habits that weren't pushing me along my highest path.

A helpful method is to free write for five to ten minutes every morning upon waking. Your mind at this point hasn't become bombarded with thoughts of the day, plans, work, worries, etc. At this time of the day, you can write energetically straight from the heart before attention moves up to the mind, where we spend most of our days. This is unconscious writing; don't think about it, just let the words flow. You can go back to the pages later to see if there are any reoccurring themes or destructive patterns you may want to begin consciously releasing.

There are many journal prompts you can use to discover the Goddess within. Pick one prompt each day. Write one sentence, one paragraph, or a whole book if you'd like! The important thing is to just get your thoughts out on paper.

40 Self Discovery Prompts

1. List five things you are grateful for today...

2. Today I feel...

3. Describe a time you felt especially valued and loved.

4. What is your greatest strength? Describe a time this strength served you well.

5. What is your greatest weakness? Describe a time you were limited by this weakness.

6. Name a book that spoke to you on a personal level. Why?

7. If you had a theme song, what would it be?

8. You feel most like yourself when...

9. Something you would love to do but you are not sure you can is...

10. What do you enjoy most about your favourite hobby? How can you incorporate that into other parts of your life?

11.   Three things you did today that moved you closer to your dreams are...

12.   Your intuition speaks to you by...

13.   If you were given $1 million dollars you would...

14.   You feel most feminine when...

15.   Describe a day in your life that was especially enjoyable. What made it so good?

16.   When you think about your future, what do you fear the most?

17.   When you think about your future, what do you hope for the most?

18.   What do you wish to attract in a partner? Do you have those characteristics?

19.   True or False: "I know how to say no and put myself first when needed." Explain.

20.   You are feeling down. What do you do to cheer yourself up?

21.   What gives you more energy: being around people or spending time alone?

22.   What are three activities that light you up and leave you feeling most energized?

23.   What is your biggest fear?

24.   What three to five qualities feel the most important for you to embody?

25.   What is the best piece of advice you've ever received?

26.   How are you most often misunderstood by other people?

27.   What are the different roles you play in your life? (e.g. mother, partner, sister, Etc.) How deeply do you identify with these roles?

28.   Who are the three most important people in your life? Why?

29.   Name one book, movie or TV show that had a profound impact on you. Why?

30.   What is one thing you look forward to every day

31.   Where do you see yourself in 10 years?

32.   What would make your teenage self proud of you now?

33.   Write a thank you letter to your body for all that it does and allows you to do.

34.   What do you look and feel like when you are most confident?

35.   Who is your hero? What makes you two relatable?

36.   If you could have dinner with five people who would they be?

37.   How do you want to be remembered?

38.   How will you make the next month a great month?

39.   What does self-love mean to you? Why is it important?

40.   What does embodying the Goddess mean to you?

Touch Yourself

Yes, you read it right. How familiar are you with your own magnificent body? Maybe this will be uncomfortable if you've never done something like this before. Maybe you've never had the time or haven't even thought to fall in love with your own touch. Your divine temple is aching to be recognized and loved by its caretaker.

1. Close the doors, take off your clothes, dim the lights, put on some soothing music and get ready to be intimate with your-Self.

2. Lay down comfortably, either on a bed or on the floor in front of a mirror, if you'd like. Close the eyes and connect to the breath for a few moments.

3. Use oil or lotion if you'd like.

4. Begin with the feet. Gently massage each, sending them love.

5. Tell them, "I love you. I appreciate you. Thank you for taking me everywhere I've been, for guiding me forward along my divine path."

6. Move up to your shins, again sending love to them, appreciating and thanking them for serving you along your path. Then up to the knees, the inner and outer thighs, take your time. Breathe into each area.

7. When you reach your *yoni* (vagina) or *lingham* (penis) area, gently touch it and the area surrounding. Rub natural, soothing oils along it. Coconut oil works well.

8. Tell this sacred area, "I love you. I appreciate you. Thank you for giving me the opportunity to connect intimately with others and to create the gift of life." Stay here as long as you'd like. If you've never spent time with this area and it makes you uncomfortable just stay for a moment then move on, spending more time here the next time you do this exercise.

9. Remember, that which we initially resist is often what we need the most. This can refer to any part of the body that feels uncomfortable or even painful to touch. Listen closely to what your body is feeling and recognize what it is saying "Yes!" to.

10. Move up to your stomach, gently rub in clockwise motions. Thanking it for the daily processes it constantly undergoes in order to keep you healthy.

11. Slowly rub up and down the sides of the body.

12. Deep, slow breathing. Moan and caress. Appreciate every touch, every inch.

13. Go to your breasts, massage them gently in circular motion. "I love you. I appreciate you." Do this for a few minutes at least. If you are a woman, meditate on how proud you are for all of the gifts that make you feminine and give you the ability to care for and nurture others.

14. Run your fingers up the sides of your necks and down the arms, thanking them for all they allow you to do.

15. Massage the hands, then each finger. "I love you. I appreciate you. Thank you."

16. Next, embrace yourself in a deep hug. Stay here for a few moments. "I love all of you. I appreciate all of you."

17. Gently massage your face in light circular motions, moving from the inward eyebrows to outward, rub the temples, glide your fingers across your lips. "You are beautiful. You are loved. You are appreciated."

18. Stay for a moment, breathing in all the loving energy that has gathered around and within your being. Stay here as long as you'd wish, appreciating the perfection that you are. If emotions come up, let them. You are safe and free to express in this space.

Dance, Darling

"Every art has its mystery, its spiritual rhythm." ~ D. T. Suzuki

These human bodies, capable of so many wonders and miracles, weren't made for sitting in front of a desk all day! They were made to move freely and limitlessly. When you let go of all inhibitions, become fully engaged in the moment and connected to the internal rhythms, movement then becomes a beautiful form of meditation. Divinity in the purest form is reflected through free, artistic expression. In these moments of pure, unadulterated creativity, our bodies become instruments for higher frequencies to flow through and guide us. This can lead to states of absolute ecstasy and joy. Not only can you experience ecstatic bliss (and what Goddess/God doesn't want that!?) but dancing is also great for overall health and emotional wellbeing. It can quickly uplift your mood by releasing feel-good endorphins, making you feel lighter, happier, and more confident within minutes. I love waking up with loud music and a little boogie around the house, it quickly shoots me into a higher vibration before conquering the day!

For those of you who are thinking, "That's great but I'm just not good at dancing." In my opinion, there is no "bad" dancing, except the dancing when you are stuck too much in your mind, and even then you can use that as an indication to what you need to work through at that time. If I'm dancing in public and notice I'm too caught up in my mind, worrying what others might think, then I know I need to spend more personal time connecting to Source and less time in my ego. Just close your eyes and move, bring your attention to the heart, and let it guide you. When you can't find the words to say, the emotions to release or you just need an escape, dance it all out. Use movement as your prayer, directly connecting you to the Divine. While Shiva is the subtle, resting potential, Shakti is here and now, nature, power and free-flowing life energy. Dancing wildly can awaken this Shakti energy, opening your portal to limitless creativity.

1. If you aren't used to dancing and feel uncomfortable doing so alone, try completing a short meditation beforehand. Ask your higher self, spirit guides, Goddess (or whichever form of Divine guidance you prefer) to allow yourself to connect to the Divine, to become an empty vessel and let it flow freely through your body, guiding each movement.

2. Light some incense or essential oils, blast your favourite song, close the eyes.

3. Move, shake, jump, shimmy and celebrate what you've got! Celebrate this life and rejoice in the fact that you have freedom to move however you wish.

4. Do it enough and eventually you'll be hooked, having impromptu solo dance parties on the regular! If you feel called to dance and connect with others look into attending local conscious, ecstatic dance events and festivals. Most importantly: Just have fun! This life's too short not to.

"When the body is calm and quiet, you can float high, you can fly high, you can become a white cloud, but only when body needs are truly looked after. The body is not your enemy, it is your friend. The body is your earth, the body has all your roots. You have to find a bridge between you and your body. If you don't find that bridge, you will be constantly in conflict with your body – and a person who is fighting with himself is always miserable. The first thing is to come to a peace-pact with your body and never break it. Once you have come to a peace-pact with your body, the body will become very, very friendly. You look after the body, the body will look after you. It becomes a vehicle of tremendous value, It becomes the very temple. One day your body itself is revealed to you as the very shrine of God."

- Osho

Creating an Altar

"That which is placed on the altar is altered." ~ Marianne Williamson

Creating a sacred space in the home is an important part of one's spiritual journey. This is a special space just for you and your practice. A sanctuary you can go to whenever you want peace, clarity, and immediate connection with the Divine. It consists of specific and sacred items meant to invite positive energy into your life. Altars are created and used by many groups around the world for religious and spiritual purposes. You can have your own and even create a communal altar available at gatherings or ceremonies. Here you can perform *sadhana* (daily spiritual practice) of meditation, *puja* (worship), offerings, *mantra, yantra* and positive affirmations. These are just suggestions, you can do whatever suits your practice and beliefs best!

Before you begin to create an altar, take time to sit in meditation and decide what you would like to clear out of your life and accept in. As you create your altar, keep these intentions in mind or perhaps write them on a piece of paper to place on the altar.

What? Choose the items that will be placed on your altar with great consideration and care. Choose any items that are sacred to you, perhaps a picture of your guru, teacher or loved ones, statues of Gods and Goddesses, candles, crystals, a written mantra, a book, sage, incense, rose petals, oracle cards, a flower, feather, rock or a seashell from a special time. Some traditions say to also add a representation of the five elements (earth, air, fire, water, space) as a way of harmonizing the nature within and around you. I keep a small bowl of water on my altar to keep the flow. Be creative. Your altar is uniquely yours.

Where? Your altar can be small or the size of an entire room! This can be anywhere you'd like, where you feel it won't be bothered or moved around. Perhaps a corner in the house or next to the area you practice yoga. They are usually made on a flat, raised surface such as a small tabletop or shelf.

When? You can go to your altar any time you feel you need to connect to Spirit, ground in or perform sadhana. Write out your thoughts and wishes, what you would like to release and put them on your altar.

How? Keep the area clean and maintained. Arrange the items however you please. The altar is meant to change and grow along with you.

Vision Board

Creating a vision board can help manifest your dreams into reality. It may sound simple, but it really works! What we focus on expands. By having your board in a sacred space where you will see it often, you are automatically practicing a visualization exercise each day. Visualization is one of the most powerful mental practices you can do. As with many meditation exercises, it can be easy to look past or forget to do our visualizations daily, but with it right in front of you that's impossible! Seeing it throughout the day and getting clear on what you want can set you in the direction of taking aligned action toward those intentions. Visualization personally changed my life. Through it I could almost see and touch the future I wanted so badly, then with newfound clarity I started making the changes needed to get there.

How does it work? The purpose of a vision board is to bring everything on it to life. If you'd like to make more than one board go ahead! Put it anywhere you know you'll see it every day. What do you want to manifest? What do you value? Think of your goals and everything you would like to accomplish in life. Don't only think of the material but the spiritual and emotional. How would you like to feel? How would you like to make others feel? How would you like to help the world?

How to create a Vision Board:

1. Gather together the following materials: A board (cork or poster board), scissors, tape, pins and/or glue stick, stickers, paint or fun markers if you'd like. Get creative! Gather magazines or books to cut images and quotes from.

2. Write out your goals on a piece of paper in the following areas: relationships, career, finances, travel, personal and spiritual growth, social life, health and home.

3. Create sacred space. Light a candle and/or incense/oils, chant, gather your crystals and play some music. If you'd like to share this experience with friends invite them over and create together!

4. Set your intention for the board. Make them be known before you begin creating.

5. Have fun! Find the images and words you'd like on your board and paste them. Make it as pretty and decorative as you'd like. Be sure to choose images that uplift you and not ones that might make you compare or feel bad about your progress.

6. Put it up somewhere you will see throughout your day. Enjoy!

Note: It's important to be aware of any resistance or obstacles that may come up while manifesting your dreams. The visuals help you stay on track, but it can't make all the necessary growth for you, know when the inner work needs to be done.

Listen to Your Heart

I honour my heart and its ability to connect with the hearts of others.
I allow love to fill me up and guide me in all my actions.
I gracefully move to the rhythm of life.

Love is our true essence, our natural vibration. It's no surprise that the energy center for love, compassion, and peace is around the heart area. The heart chakra, *Anahata*, resides in the center of the chest. This is why at times we can feel a physical heart ache or strong, loving emotions wash over this area. The physical and energetic bodies, matter and consciousness, Shakti and Shiva, are constantly dancing and making love to each other at each chakra. The *Anahata* is a crucial energy center where many physical and energetic pathways interact—it is the bridge between the lower, physical chakras and the upper, spiritual chakras.

Through life's struggles and perhaps heartbreaks, we may over time unconsciously close off to others and even to ourselves. We literally build energetic walls over our hearts, guarding our ability to love and be loved. When this happens, the *Anahata* can become blocked. This can also affect our self-esteem as we begin to lose self-love. When you let go of pains from your past, you slowly begin to open again and find an expanded space in which you can step into compassion and joy.

Personally, I was skeptical of chakras and the energy bodies when I first began my spiritual quest. Coming from a scientific background, it was hard for me to believe in this new system that couldn't be measured. For many years after my abusive relationships I stopped crying, I stopped feeling altogether. I was emotionally numb without realizing it. When I did make a connection and shared intimately with another, they would often comment how cold I was afterwards. I didn't want to be touched and definitely didn't want to hold hands! That sounded revolting to me at the time.

I started seeing energy healers in different countries and was surprised to hear the same thing from each, that there was no energy flowing around my heart, I had an energetic blockage. One even compared me to a vampire! It took a lot of work and strong intention but finally, with the help of an incredible medicine woman, my heart reopened. After many deep sessions with her I remained emotionless, but one night after a deep massage, opening up more about my past, she brought me on a journey through sound healing. As she hit the Tibetan sound bowl loudly over my heart center, finally it opened. BAM! It wasn't graceful, it was messy. I cried, screamed and felt like a weight had been lifted off of my chest that I never knew was there. The woman held me as I let it all out. After that things changed, I changed, and I trusted in the power of energy healing.

As you will learn in the section on chakras, a blocked heart chakra can lead to feelings of being unloved, as though it's hard to love others and yourself, loneliness, jealousy, insecurity, judgement of others or yourself, and being emotionally distant. These can also manifest into physical symptoms such as hypertension, problems breathing, infection at the level of the lung, bronchitis, and heart conditions. At the other end, your heart can be too open, causing you to love too much and possibly be hurt because of it, constantly feeling like a victim, losing sense of personal boundaries and being overly demanding of a partner or others. I went from one extreme to the next. The key, as always, is balance. Have an open heart but still keep it safe. Be vulnerable yet protect your feelings. Love deeply while respecting personal boundaries.

Remember to be gentle with yourself along the heart opening journey. Honor the process. It's normal to not be in complete alignment all of the time, that's how we grow!

Listen to your heart meditation:

1. Sit or lay somewhere you feel comfortable and safe. Place a healing crystal on the heart chakra if you'd like.

2. Close the eyes. For just a moment let go of all thoughts of the outside world.

3. Begin to breathe into the heart centre, visualizing a healing green light energy building all around it. This light might be rotating or spiralling as energy begins to grow in this area.

4. It's glowing cleaner and brighter with every inhale, cleansing this sacred space.

5. Feel your old pain and guilt wash away with each exhale.

6. Inhale love, exhale anything that no longer serves you. Anything weighing you down, literally giving you a heavy heart. Anything that might be holding you back from opening your heart to giving and receiving love fully.

7. After about 10 breaths, place your hands over your heart centre, and ask your heart what it has to say. This isn't an order but rather an intention that you'd like the heart to express itself.

8. For the next 5 to 15 minutes listen to what the heart has to express and is ready to let go of. Allow fears, memories, wishes and dreams to come and go naturally. Don't try to push any away, honour it all, then let it go gracefully.

9. If you need to cry then cry. If you need to laugh then laugh! Let this experience be what it is. If your mind wanders, simply bring your attention back to heart center.

10. When you feel ready repeat a divine affirmation to end. Such as, *"I am divine and am a perfect embodiment of love" "I can love myself and others, as I am them and they are me"* or *"I am healing and opening my heart to the love I deserve".*

11. You may wish to record in your journal what the heart had to say so you can look back at it later.

If clear emotions don't come up the first time, continue this exercise every day until you see and feel with clarity. Each day you will become more connected with your heart.

"Deep within all of you lays this primal power, an unstoppable primal force. Chaotic and uncontrollable, teeming with life and overflowing passion, this power hides in the darkness, the mystery of creation between form and formless. It is from here that all life pours in an inexhaustible torrent." ~ *Womb Wisdom: Awakening the Creative and Forgotten Powers of the Feminine*

Wisdom from the Womb

When was the last time you connected with your womb? It is recognized in numerous cultures that a woman's womb is the seat of her wisdom, creativity, inspiration, and power. Yet, somewhere along the way the modern woman has lost touch with this sacred space. We pay little attention to it except during pregnancy or menstruation, the rest of the time it's usually neglected. When I began to strongly disconnect from my womb space, I started to have severe menstrual pains that left me bed-ridden. I saw this as a message from the Divine Mother to tune back into my sacred space and listen to what it has to say. Rather than taking painkillers, you might want to listen closely during your next menstruation. Is your womb trying to get your attention? What is it asking for?

This powerful, creative energy is also present in men and can be found in the same region. In many ancient traditions it's said our belly holds our personal power and life energy. This energy is stored around the lower chakras in high amounts as it contains the catalyst for life in men and the space for life to be created in women.

The stomach's corresponding element is Earth, and just as Earth nurtures and cares for all of us, the stomach cares for and powers all of the other organs. Because this is such a significant region of the body, men can practice a similar exercise as below while meditating on their lower stomach.

"Science is now discovering that more neutrons fire in our bellies than our actual brains. There are in fact 72,000 nerve endings in our bellies, whereas only 50, 000 are found within the brain. In Chinese medicine, the small intestine (part of the womb circuit) is the place that stores the deeper emotional issues from our hearts, and in Tibetan medicine it is the center for affection and bonding." -Womb Wisdom: Awakening the Creative and Forgotten Powers of the Feminine

For women, our womb is what makes us divinely feminine. Unfortunately, society today has taught most of us to be ashamed of our femininity, causing us to disconnect from our bodies. As women we have the capability to create outside of our bodies as well as within. That is nothing less than an absolute miracle! Something so marvellous and magical we can't even begin to fully understand with our human brains. Something that we should take pride in and celebrate. We have put away our needs and desires for too long. When we reawaken the Goddess within, we empower ourselves while setting an example for the future generations of Goddesses who come after. The evolved woman regards herself and all others as sacred, she honours her intuition and listens to her innate, womb wisdom. When we disconnect from our womb space and it becomes unbalanced, our emotions may be difficult to control, creativity is blocked, fertility is impaired, libido is lowered, and troubles begin to pop up in personal relationships. You may also experience physical pain in that region and have a difficult menstruation. This is a calling to bring your attention inward. The womb is not to be neglected or shamed; it is the gatekeeper of the secrets to the universe and all of life.

If you've created your sacred altar, put some special items that represent the womb and the divine feminine to you, if you haven't already. This is a reminder to celebrate and be proud of your feminine essence. Wear a blessed piece of jewelry when you're on your moon cycle as another reminder of this time's sacredness. When was the last time you looked at your own blood? Honor your flow when it comes, rather than shying away from it. Acknowledge the emotions that come up and let them be expressed. Try to use natural feminine products and never douche, as this can destroy the good bacteria within. While I understand many women feel they must use contraceptive pills, I encourage you to explore more natural options. Respect and care for your *yoni*, your sacred portal. Celebrate that you are a woman, capable of so many miracles! Once the gentle care and recognition has taken place, then we can reconnect with our womb through meditation. By connecting with the womb, we connect with Mother Earth while beginning to explore what energies, emotions, and past experiences or traumas are being held here. As we did with our hearts, we must listen closely to the voice of the womb. Your womb will let you know how she wants to be loved and healed.

1. Get comfortable in your sacred space. Laying down in Goddess pose, touching the bottoms of both feet together while forming a diamond shape with the legs. Use a blanket or pillow if needed.

2. Rest your hands over your womb space.

3. Plant a seed of intention and light within your womb. How would you like to gain and grow from this experience? How will you nurture and water this seed afterwards?

4. Connect with the breath for a few minutes. Inhaling and exhaling deeply and fully. Bringing your attention to the stomach, then to the womb. Breathe into this area. Allow your exhale to be slightly longer than the inhale, relaxing the body. Notice the pause between breaths, direct your attention there. Rest in knowing you are safe and divinely protected in this space and time.

5. Place your hands in the *yoni mudra* above the womb. Thumbs and index fingers touch while the back fingers curl in.

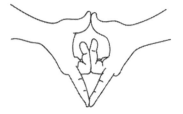

6. Breathe in her wisdom and cosmic light. Ask your womb if there is anything she would like to share with you. Listen without judgement. Observe without attachment.

7. Honor whatever emotions may come arise and let them be released.

8. Imagine or feel roots growing from your womb down to Mother Earth. Through the soil, rock and hot magma. All the way to the center where a beautiful, pure crystal quartz lays. Wrap your roots around this healing quartz. Absorb her healing and grounding energies into your roots and back up to your womb. Allow her to absorb all the pain or negative energies you hold on to, she can absorb as much as you give her without becoming affected. Feel centered and balanced. Allow her maternal, nurturing energy to heal you.

9. When you feel you have absorbed all of the energy you need, slowly bring awareness back to your body. Watch the breath.

10. Allow your breathing to return to normal. Thank your womb for all that it does, and all it is capable of doing. Thank Mother for watching over you, protecting and nurturing you. You may wish to repeat an affirmation before closing this meditation.

Womb Affirmations:

My womb is sacred. My womb is divine.
My womb is love. My womb is whole.
My womb is healed. My womb is free.
My womb is radiant. My womb is light.
My womb is celestial. My womb is bliss.
My womb is liberated. My womb is full of energy.
My womb is pure. My womb is all powerful.
My womb is the seat of my creativity and wisdom.

Yoni Egg

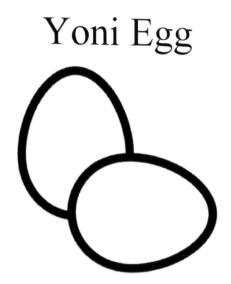

Yoni means sacred space and is the symbol of Shakti, the great Goddess, in Hinduism. Today we often use this word to refer to the vagina, here I will be using it in that context. The yoni egg, Jade egg or love egg is a semiprecious stone carved into the shape of an egg and polished to be worn inside the yoni. Sometimes it has a string attached for easy removal. The first known use of yoni eggs was in the Royal Palaces of ancient China. Empresses and concubines used them to awaken sensuality, access sexual power and preserve their youth.

Some practices believe that the strength of a woman's pelvic floor muscles directly influence how old she looks and feels. Using an egg made of Jade is usually preferred for its many properties such as increasing balance, wisdom, stamina, peace and harmony. If you feel called to use other stones that's fine too, Rose Quartz, Black Obsidian and Amethyst are also popularly used. It's important to listen to your yoni then decide if you'd like to try the egg or not. It can be a great tool to bring attention and love back to the yoni. Personally the egg helped me deeply to reconnect with my yoni after sexual trauma.

Benefits of Using the Yoni Egg:

- Recovery after childbirth
- Increased libido
- Enhanced sexual pleasure
- Reduced menstrual cramps
- More intense orgasms
- Balancing feminine and masculine energies
- Helps discover and love your body more deeply
- Metaphysical properties of the individual gemstones & crystals
- Preventing or remedying urinary incontinence
- Easier childbirth
- Stronger vaginal muscles
- Balance estrogen levels

Choosing your size: Yoni eggs mainly come in three sizes: small, medium, and large. The smaller the egg the less you will feel. Just because it's a small egg doesn't mean it's for a small woman. Generally, women who have given birth or have gone through menopause should try a larger egg to begin. Otherwise medium is usually your best bet. If you still think you can go smaller after trying the medium, change to small after a week or two of use.

How to use: First you must clear and cleanse the egg. You can do this by boiling it in water with a pinch of sea salt for at least ten minutes. You can then sage around it with your intentions for its usage in mind or leave it in a glass of natural water under the light of the full moon or sun. I bring mine into the mountains and energize it in the pure mountain springs before use.

Connect with your egg: Before you begin to use it, infuse it with your energy and intention. Meditate with your egg close to your heart and womb, holding it and even speaking your intentions to it. Place it on your sacred altar during puja. Sleep with it next to you.

Introduce your egg to your yoni: Set aside some time alone in your sacred space. Turn on some relaxing music. You may want to perform the Touch Yourself ritual before inserting the egg. You can place light coconut oil on your egg and gently rub it around your yoni with your intention in mind before inserting. Use a mirror to connect more deeply. Once it is in meditate on this space for a few moments. How do you want the egg to help in your healing journey? What do you wish to gain from using this special tool?

It's in! Now what? Although doing Kegel exercises will enhance your experience, the yoni egg is beneficial by simply just wearing it. To begin try leaving it in for about two hours, three to four times per week. Don't leave it in for longer than twelve hours, after that take it out and clean it while letting your yoni rest. Be careful to listen gently and honour how your yoni feels. If you find that you have trouble holding the egg in throughout the day then try sitting with the egg inside a few times a week for 15 minutes or so to start. Over time your strength will increase so you can hold it in while walking about.

It's recommended to not use the egg during your moon cycle, while pregnant or with any internal infection.

Note: This is a short introduction to the yoni egg, please conduct your own research as well as consult with a medical professional before using.

Sacred Sensuality

"When you have sex, take with you to bed only love and senses, all five of them. Only then will you experience communion with god." Paulo Coelho, 'Brida'

How often do we overlook the beautiful gift of the senses? Rather than being ignorant why don't we embrace their presence and indulge in these pleasures with true appreciation? In Tantra, we honour each sense as a gateway into expanded consciousness. How blessed are we to have the opportunity to smell the flowers we walk by, to hear a child's laugh, to see Earth's unending beauty, to experience the unique tastes from around the world, to gently touch the ones we love? We have so much to learn from our sensorial experience of life.

Sacred sensuality is fully embracing this present moment and all it has to offer. Shakti (physical manifestation) can be used as a direct pathway to reach Shiva (higher consciousness). A Tantric Goddess finds pleasure, bliss and meditative states through the sacred senses all day long. Along with the following morning puja, begin to embrace the senses throughout the day. See their pleasures as a direct invitation from the Divine to realize eternity and bliss through this present moment. Be aware of the beautiful flowers as you walk down the street, slowly take in their fragrance, run your fingers gently over them, witness their vibrant colors. Count how many beautiful things you see in a day, whether it be nature, a friendly face, or a helping hand. Let everything you do be filled with appreciation and love. Falling madly in love with the senses allows you to fall madly in love with your-Self, as they are part of you! Remember, you are an absolute miracle, a child of the cosmos, connected to everything small and big. Fully recognize and experience your gifts.

Puja means to worship, and this particular puja is a morning practice for bringing awareness and gratitude to the senses. Now that you have your sacred altar space prepared you can begin a beautiful daily practice. It is recommended to perform this puja for forty days, preferably in the morning upon waking. Sitting in front of the altar, make an offering to the senses. We do this by using an item that stimulates each one. We offer this item by waving it three times vertically in a clockwise direction to the altar, then bowing to the Divine (Spirit, your higher Self, etc.) Each of the senses has a corresponding element and chakra. You may wish to place a hand on the chakra of the sense you are working with and breathe into it.

Smell (Earth, Muladhara):
Offer an aroma that is particularly arousing to you,
perhaps a flower petal or incense.

Taste (Water, Svadistana):
Offer a delicious food and take a small bite, taking in the full range of flavours,
perhaps some berries or a small chocolate.

Sight (Fire, Manipura):
Offer a candle or light incense and watch the flame,
contemplating the fire for a moment.

Touch: (Air, Anahata):

Offer an item particularly soothing to the touch such as silk cloth or soft lotion, touch it and rub it gently against your skin.

Hearing (Ether, Vishuddha):

Offer your positive affirmation or a sacred mantra aloud.

*(The highest two chakras do not have a physical form
as they are beyond the elements).*

The offerings can be visual or real, depending on what you have available on the given day. You can also use an item for more than one sense, such as a flower for touch, smell and sight. Once you have completed this puja you may wish to meditate with the senses in mind, using them as a connection to this present moment. Give thanks for this physical existence.

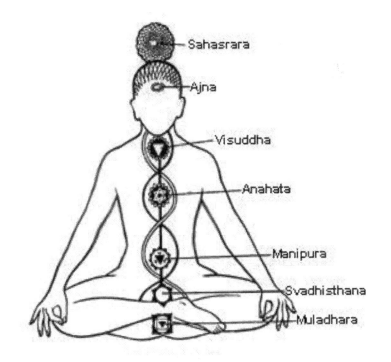

Essential Oils

Essential oils are a delicious and uplifting component to add to your rituals, meditations, yoga and overall wellness. The healing power of plants has been around for thousands of years and can allow you to have a much deeper experience in your practice. Essential oils are highly concentrated oils with a yummy aroma that are extracted directly from the bark, flower, fruit, leaf, seed or root of a plant or tree. They can be used as a sacred tool to immediately connect back to nature, even if you are in the middle of the city. It is important in Goddess practices to dive deep into all of the sacred senses, especially that of smell. It is said that smell is the strongest of the senses for memory, so find your favourite aroma and as you take it all in let it bring you back to beautiful thoughts and memories. Just one drop can also have powerful health benefits, quickly uplift your mood and strengthen concentration. You can use essential oils in self-care products such as shampoos, moisturizers and lip balm. They can also be used orally, in a diffuser, added to massage oil or in the bath (just make sure to read the label first). I almost always begin my day or a meditation by smelling eucalyptus for clarity and end my day with lavender for relaxation. They can be used as a wonderful offering for the sense of smell in the Sacred Sensuality puja! Make sure you use high quality oils that are made specifically for how you'd like to use them. Experiment with different oils and blends to find your favs!

My Personal Favourites:

Rose: This aroma always makes me feel immediately feminine. It's incredible for reducing skin inflammation and creating healthy, glowing skin. Add a few drops to your facial moisturizer!

Sandalwood: Sandalwood has been considered sacred all around the world for thousands of years. It's known to increase concentration in meditation, improve libido, soothe anxiety and insomnia and even send spirits to heaven after death.

Rosemary: Can naturally thicken hair, so it's great to add to homemade shampoos. Also, it improves brain function and memory so it's great to use when working, reading or studying.

Tea Tree Oil: A natural anti-bacterial, anti-fungal, fights infection, reduces bad odours and can help stimulate the immune system. Good to use in a room while sick or healing.

Lavender: Helps with relaxation, sleeping problems, improves mood and heals burns and cuts.

Grapefruit/Lemon/Orange: Supports metabolism and cellulite reduction. Mix with coconut oil and rub on areas of cellulite or take a few drops internally with water. Citrus fruits in general instantly uplift the mood and leave you feeling fresh. I love having grapefruit and orange in my soaps for a morning boost!

Smudging

Smudging refers to the powerful cleansing and purifying technique, the sacred smoke bowl blessing, that's believed to have been used traditionally by Native Americans for centuries. It's created by bundling together a selection of herbs, often sage, with string to form a smudge stick before being ignited. Most ancient cultures also have their own form of cleansing and blessing rituals. This can be seen today most commonly by an incense burning in a church or temple or a medicine man's sacred bowl of smudge.

The spirits of healing plants are called upon to restore balance and drive away negative energies. How does it work? We are much more than just these physical bodies and our homes are much more than just a space we live, each have many invisible energies floating around from people and objects of the present and past. Cleansing a space or body clears built up negative energy or emotions. If you don't believe it try for yourself, quite often there is a noticeable shift in energy right after smudging! It can quickly turn a regular home into a soothing and uplifting sanctuary. The herbs most often used in smudge sticks are sage and sweet grass, both being powerful tools for driving out negative energies, influences and spirits. It's also believed to release negative ions, which has been linked in studies to a more positive mood (higher serotonin levels) and overall wellness. In high enough concentrations, negative ions can clear the air of mold, dust, odors, cigarette smoke, bacteria, and viruses. Most of us are saturated in positive ions from the technology, radio signals, electronics, air conditioning, heaters and pollution we are constantly surrounded by. Negative ions that occur from smudging can be beneficial in counteracting these effects. Smudging is like taking an energetic shower! Sweetgrass, or holy grass, is a sacred plant from North America, it's often burned after sage or other plants in ceremony.

What You Will Need: Smudge stick & Small ceramic/stone bowl or large shell.

How to Smudge:

1. As always, set an intention before you begin.

2. Connect to Spirit through prayer and give thanks for the plants and the earth that gifts them to us.

3. Ignite the plant, let it burn for 20-30 seconds before blowing it out as smoke is produced.

4. Purify yourself and others if present with the smoke. Some prefer to go head to heart and down to the feet, but you can do it however you like!

5. If purifying a space, walk slowly around, wafting the smoke to each corner and all around. I personally like to sing a protecting mantra at this time.

6. Burn sweetgrass if you have some prepared.

7. Put the stick out using your bowl of choice and later once the ashes cool, return them to the earth, once again thanking the plants.

You can also add a large feather to waft the smudge, aromatherapy, essential oils and bells, drums or rattles, crystals and candles (fire is said to be deeply purifying and transformational).

"Every woman who heals herself helps heal all the women who came before her and all those who will come after.
~ Dr. Christiane Northrup

Conscious Eating

"Many people are not aware of how large of an effect their diet has on their state of being. Your physiological health is literally the platform for your consciousness. The Nero-transmitters and hormones responsible for your moods and state of being are directly correspondent to your nutritional intake, as well as the level of toxins that are present in your system. You are what you eat and if you're eating dead chemical filled junk, you will feel like dead chemical filled junk..." ~ Patrick Haize

In almost every culture, food has long played a significant physical, social and spiritual role, it's become much more than a means of survival. Food brings families and communities together, heals the sick and gives us the energy to live. Food is medicine! We have been given all the means to survive and flourish by consuming natural, fresh foods from the earth. I met elders from the jungles who told me their jungle is the only supermarket and pharmacy they'll ever need. When you really think about it, it simply makes sense not to put chemicals or man-made prescriptions into our temples, the earth has provided us with all we need. Not only are natural, high vibrational foods better for our bodies but they're also better for the planet, our home. Surely an apple picked off a tree that will continue to live and offer us its juicy gifts afterwards is much more sustainable than picking up a slab of decomposing meat from the local grocery store that carries unnecessary death with it.

A high vibrational diet consists of foods that are ALIVE and that positively benefit the person, as well as the planet as a whole. High vibration means having more light, less density and packed full of nutrients. Plants exemplify this by photosynthesizing light into energy. Yes, I'm vegan. I have been for twelve years, but I'm not writing to push this lifestyle choice onto anyone. For I know in my heart that those who practice the rituals in this book with true intention over a significant period of time will naturally want to put the healthiest and highest quality ingredients into their temple body. I once attended a speech by a popular Swami and there were some young kids in the audience. One asked the Swami, "So are you saying that in order for us to follow a lifestyle similar to you we have to become vegetarian?" The swami chuckled, "No, you don't even have to think about being vegetarian. For after you begin to follow these exercises and look deep within, you will naturally stop supporting the suffering of other beings. You will know that we are all connected, like you are my brother so is the cow or sheep."

We aren't speaking about the few places in the world that actually rely on animal meat to survive. I'm from Canada, I know there are places far North that simply don't have the luxury of fresh produce and grains all year round. In that case we must adapt or move. Those elders from the jungle ate meat when they needed to, only killing one animal to feed their family for days. During the process they prayed and thanked the animal spirit for blessing them with the ability to survive. What we see in the meat and dairy industries nowadays is nothing close to natural or for means of survival. In most parts of the world however, nature has gifted us an abundance high vibrational foods that are full of life. Unfortunately in today's society with the rise of fast and convenient foods, eating has become quite often a mindless act. There is no gratitude for food when you're quickly scarfing it down in the car on your way to work or eating a muffin running down the street to your next meeting.

Over time we have lost our connection to food and the act of eating has lost its sacredness. Below are some general tips I personally use to honor my temple body and what I put into it. I also encourage you to explore local farms, farmer's markets and small grocers. Many believe that eating a healthy diet is more expensive and that's rarely the case. If you eat meat and dairy you will notice most of the time those are the most expensive items on your receipt.

When I was a broke student I contacted farms and asked if I could offer a little volunteering in exchange for fresh fruit and produce. Think outside the box! It's much better to invest in yourself now rather than pay medical bills later.

"If the taste is not lived, you are just stuffing. Go slow, and be aware of the taste. And only when you go slow can you be aware. Do not just go on swallowing things. Taste them unhurriedly and become the taste. When you feel the sweetness, become that sweetness. And then it can be felt all over the body — not just in the mouth, not just on the tongue, it can be felt all over the body! A certain sweetness — or anything else — is spreading in ripples. Whatsoever you are eating, feel the taste and become the taste. This is how Tantra appears to be quite the contrary from other traditions." ~ Osho

Tips for Eating Consciously:

1. Chew your food! Enjoy every bite. Feel appreciative for this energetic exchange. This goes back to our practice of embracing the senses. Taste every flavour. Meditate on it until you are in a state of absolute sensory pleasure! Mmmmm.

2. As you chew imagine where that food has come from and all the processes it took to reach your mouth!

3. Don't overcook your grains or veggies. This kills the nutrients and changes the vibration. Choose raw plants whenever you have the option.

4. Cook for yourself whenever you can. This allows for deeper connection with the food. Appreciate each ingredient as you prepare it for cooking, mentally thanking the tree or soil it may have come from.

5. Sit down for each meal. Turn off the TV. Respect your food. Make it an event! Carving out the extra ten minutes to sit down and truly enjoy the flavours you are putting into your body is well worth it.

6. Enjoy the foods you crave in small amounts rather than becoming upset with yourself for indulging. You shouldn't feel deprived when following a healthy, nutritious diet. Personally, I love chocolate so I keep my favourite dark chocolate in the fridge with my vitamins and have a small piece every day. I keep it with my vitamins so I feel like I'm doing something good for my body when I reach for a piece. That way it doesn't come with the guilt that used to lead to overeating and "falling off the wagon".

7.   Create a short prayer of gratitude before every meal. Once you do this for a week or two it will become habit. Mine is usually something like this: "Thank you Earth for gifting me with this meal. Thank you to those who farmed these beautiful ingredients, packaged and cooked them (if I'm eating outside of home), bless each of them. May we (everyone in the world) have no shortage of food one day." Sometimes I will include a mantra of the Hindu God or Goddess I am working with at the time in my prayer of gratitude.

8. Learn what cravings mean, they come to be for a reason! They are important memos from the body to tell us what needs to change. This could be a nutrient you are missing or even an emotion you are ignoring.

About a year ago I had a miscarriage, and shortly after I put on extra weight. I had been craving high carbs and fatty foods, filling foods. It wasn't until I recognized that I was looking to fill my stomach, as it felt empty after losing the little spirit that was once there, in order to comfort myself from the pain. Once I dealt with the pain I naturally lost the gained weight.

This is a more extreme example, but here are some others:

- We can crave salty foods out of fear.
- We want to have more "spice" in our lives but are too afraid to take risks.
- We tend to overeat high gluten or wheat products for comfort and safety, or not to feel so "empty" or alone.
- Sugar cravings can come when we are excited or if we have no one to share our excitement with.

- Cravings for dairy may come when we are actually craving unconditional love and protection, just like the milk we received from our mothers.

If you want to protect yourself from the world you may crave fatty foods. This is literally protecting us (with fat layers) from others. And the most important thing to remember is to simply listen to your body! Tune in and ask it what it wants. Being mindful is simply being present and in tune with your body, mind and spirit.

Goddess Bathing

Ready for some magic!? Personally, nothing leaves me feeling as uplifted in a short amount of time as a beautiful bath meant for a Goddess/God. You guessed it; washing yourself can be another form of blissful meditation while connecting more deeply with your sacred (naked) temple! The best part of bath supplies is that they are usually quite cheap, so splurge a little! Make your bathroom sacred and as luxurious as any spa, for a quarter of the price. The best part is that this is your own sacred space that you can come to anytime you want. If you don't have a bathtub you can place candles all around and have a steamy hot shower to your favourite uplifting music or simply soak your feet in a bowl with some of the following ingredients.

Suggested items for Making a Magic Bath:

- Candles
- Essential oils
- Coconut oil
- Natural healing salts
- Natural bath bomb
- Yummy, relaxing music
- Flower petals
- Loofa or small towel
- Pieces of your favourite fruit (for inside the bath or to snack on!)
- Herbal tea (to drink)

Stress-Relieving Bath Recipe: 2 cups Epsom Salt, 1 cup Baking Soda, 1/2 cup Himalayan Salt, Rosemary, Grapefruit/Lavender oils or Dried Lavender Flowers

Your Ritual:

1. Run your bath (or fill your bowl if you're enjoying a foot soak).
2. Dim the lights, light some candles, diffuse your favourite, most soothing essential oils, and play relaxing music that you absolutely love. Make this a sexy celebration of the senses!
3. Add all of the delicious ingredients into the water with the intention of taking this moment entirely for yourself, for relaxation, connection and empowerment.
4. Soak for at least 10 minutes, closing the eyes and taking it all in through each of the senses.
5. Grab your loofa or small towel and beginning from the feet, slowly massage your body. Sending each part love and gratitude. Take your time. You may

want to spend more time in some parts of the body than others and that's fine. Let this experience be your own.

6.   Sip some herbal tea during the process! Chamomile is always a good choice. When I finish my tea I throw the bag in the tub for extra benefits!

7.   When you are ready to step out of your soak, dry off and take your time massaging your skin with your favourite body oil or lotion.

Forest Bathing

"A walk in nature walks the soul back home." ~ Mary Davis

Forest Bathing or Nature Therapy, is the medicine of simply being in the forest. The Japanese have been using it as a method of preventative health care and healing since the 1980s. Growing up in the mountains, I have intuitively used this technique my entire life. Any time I've felt lost or confused about my direction in life I've gone into the forest for at least one full day alone. The forest heals not only on the physical level; lowering stress and improving overall health, but also on emotional and spiritual levels. The trees and earth can be so nurturing, it's no wonder she is our Mother. Nature can be our greatest teacher, whether it's learning how to change gracefully like the leaves, flow freely like the water or how to live in harmony like so many of the animals, there's always something new to take in if you are open to learning. After traveling extensively, I have witnessed a great deal of destruction and disrespect to our Mother Earth. I often wonder, if everyone did this exercise and was truly alone in nature a little bit each day, would our environment still be treated the same? There is no denying our deep love and connection to nature after spending time with it, this should be met with gratitude and awe, rather than ignorance and destruction.

How does it work? Forest bathing is very simple: Be in the presence of trees. That's it! If you don't live near a forest any nature nearby will work. Here we are reconnecting with our Mother, and she is always there to listen, teach and love you. Breathe deeply and allow her wisdom to direct you. She is always whispering to you, story-telling and sharing secrets of the past. Appreciate and fully experience the trees, dance to the sounds of leaves blowing in the wind, run barefoot through the flowers and lay directly on the earth, absorbing all her healing energy. I like to sing sacred mantras to the trees and meditate on all the things they must have seen in their wise years. Leave your shoes at home and walk or dance barefoot on the earth. As mentioned with smudging, the earth sends negative ions through our feet, healing and rejuvenating us! We have shoes on so often that we block this important exchange, so run free through the dirt, mud, or sand whenever you have the chance!

"So powerful is the light of unity that it can illuminate the whole earth." ~ Bahá'u'lláh

Moon Rituals

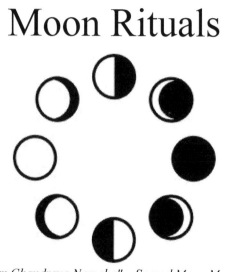

"Om Chandraya Namaha" ~ Sacred Moon Mantra

Just as connecting with the feminine power of Mother Earth is so important to an awakening Goddess, so is remaining aligned with the moon. It has the power to change tides, and since we are around 70% water, we are highly connected with the magical, mysterious Mama Moon. You'll notice women especially are remembering their powerful relationship to the different phases of the moon. Begin to pay attention to which phase falls on each day, perhaps have a reminder on your phone. Once you begin to get in tune with the Moon's cycles, you begin to connect deeply with the cosmos and nature. Choosing to tap into the energy of the moon can add an element of new beauty, mystery, and flow to life. This can bring awareness to other cycles and rhythms within your own body, mind and spirit. Try these rituals for each new moon and full moon to begin reconnecting and aligning deeply with the moon. Personally, I like to plan the rituals and take a Goddess bath beforehand.

New Moon: New Beginnings

1. The new moon is the perfect time to assess what needs to change in your life and to create NEW intentions to act upon. What do you wish to manifest in this next month?

2. Find a sacred space, being outside under the moon if possible is best.

3. Smudge the area with your intentions in mind.

4. Set up an altar with all of your favourite sacred items. Lay your crystals to recharge, use items that connect you with nature: a feather, flower or seashell for example.

5. Make a fire in this sacred space. Light candles if an outdoor fire isn't possible. Fire represent transformation, change and new beginnings.

6. Prepare beforehand a paper with all your desires. What you would like to manifest? What would you like to ask the universe for? You might want to begin the paper with something like, "I accept the following into my life for my highest good and the highest good of all.."

7. Now you may want to begin by offering gratitude to the Earth and Moon, and acknowledge the elements. Say your intentions for this new moon. Read out your desires. Include a poem, song or instrument that helps to set the energy. If you are performing this ritual with others allow them to speak their intentions.

8. Burn the paper with your intentions. Fire also represents action, know that these wishes will be put into action as you watch it burn. You may wish to meditate or write in a journal how you will put these desires into action within the following month.

9. During the following weeks be aware of your intentions and the work you are doing to reach them. Record them in your journal if you'd like.

Full Moon: Letting Go

It is a time to release that which no longer serves your highest purpose; what you no longer need in your life or an aspect of yourself that you have outgrown. The moon energy is powerful and intense. This surge enables you to take action – especially in regards to the New Moon intentions you may have made two weeks prior. The full moon is the time to let go of anything that has been weighing you down or holding you back from living the life of your dreams. Do you feel heavy? Is there any pain, resentment, jealousy or anger you may be holding on to? It's time to release all that no longer serves your highest path.

Repeat steps 1-4 of the full moon ritual.

1. Prepare beforehand a paper with everything you'd like to release from your life. Meditate on your fears, small or big and write them down. Think of any attachments you may have, any expectations. Any blockages or anything getting in the way of you reaching your goals and living the life of your dreams.

2. Again, acknowledge the elements, the Earth and Moon, and your Divine guides of choice. Ask them to help you lose the following from your life in order to live your highest good. Read out all of the things you want to release. Some examples may be: Fear of change, comparing yourself to others, holding on to past lovers, seeking approval from others, releasing a job or relationship, old limiting beliefs, clinging onto things, unhealthy expectations, the need to control, jealousy, resentment from the past, worries of the future, the belief you are not good enough, childhood wounds, financial worries.

3. Follow with a poem, song or instrument that helps to set the energy. If you are performing this ritual with others now allow them to share what they wish to release from their own lives.

4. You may wish to burn the paper, rip it into pieces, send it down streaming water or roll it up and tie it to a balloon, watching it float away. Do any action that represents releasing to you.

5. Thank your guides or higher self for helping you along your divine path by giving you strength to recognize that which is no longer is serving you and the courage to release it.

6. During the following weeks be aware of any fears or things you'd like to release popping up, and gracefully let it go. Record this in your journal if you'd like.

Note: You may wish to perform the meditation in the Letting Go section during the full moon ritual or later if having issues releasing.

*"Let us fall in love again
and scatter gold dust all over the world.
Let us become a new spring
and feel the breeze drift in heaven's scent.
Let us dress the earth in green
and like the sap of a young tree
let the grace from within us sustain us.
Let us carve gems out of our stony hearts
and let them light our path to Love.
The glance of Love is crystal clear
and we are blessed by its light."
~ Rumi*

Healing Crystals

Crystals have their own unique vibrations and can be used for healing, ceremony and overall wellbeing. They are often referred to as "wisdom keepers" because they hold the Earth's history and secrets of the centuries within them. While stones from the earth have been used since ancient times, today you can find them everywhere from stores, spas, infused in beauty products and as decor in homes. A great way to harness their power is by using healing stones for manifesting your intentions and what you want to create in your life. Crystals connect us to the Earth because they are tangible, physical forms that have powerful vibrations. This energy continues to connect with you when you wear these intention crystals close to the skin or place them in your environment. With every thought and intention, these crystals pick up on your unique vibrational energy and amplify the positive vibes you are cultivating.

In this magical world of vibrations, crystal energy helps you on your spiritual journey because it works to hold your intention and remind you of your connection to the Earth. Albert Einstein said everything in life is vibration, and just like sound waves, your thoughts match the vibrations of everything that manifests in your life. Therefore, if you think crystals have healing potential, the positive vibes of the stones will amplify those thoughts. Not only are they beautiful and make you feel good, certain types of crystals have specific qualities.

Choosing: Once you know the crystal basics, use your intuition to choose the right healing stones for your spiritual journey. Crystal experts often say that the crystal chooses you instead of the other way around. Walk around the store and see what crystals stand out to you. Whether it's the dazzling colors, shapes or patterns that draw you in, each crystal has a unique energy that works to clear blockages and ward off negative energy. If you are well connected with Spirit and Earth, you may intuitively know which one is for you at that time in your life. Hold the stone in your hand and quietly think of your intention. Notice if you feel sensations such as hot or cold, pulsations, or calmness and tranquility. These are all signs that this particular rock is perfect for your healing needs.

Cleansing: Once you have chosen your crystal, it's important that you cleanse it to clear away the energy of where it's been before you and all the hands it may have touched. You can cleanse your crystal by running it through natural spring waters then placing it under the sun or moon for 24 hours, infusing it with sacred smoke from smudging or placing it in a room with high vibrational music playing.

How to Use:

1. Set your intention after cleansing, speaking or saying mentally what you'd like to receive from your special crystal. Use your intuition when deciding which way of using the crystal is best for you. You can use it: During healing, around or on the body/chakras, meditation, near you during yoga

2. On your altar, during ceremonies you may wish to use different types of stones for different rooms in the home, such as a protection stone in the bedroom or concentration stone in the office

3. Carry it around with you in your pocket or purse to have its powerful qualities at all times

4.Use it as jewelry or put in pillow

5. Exchange. I like to give crystals that have soaked up my energy to loved ones

Great Crystals to Start With:

- Rose quartz for unconditional love
- Amethyst for spiritual awareness and safe travels
- Turquoise for healing
- Carnelian for creativity
- Clear Quartz for meditation
- Aventurine for confidence and self-worth
- Citrine for abundance
- Black Tourmaline for grounding

"She's already had everything she needs within herself. It's the world that's convinced her she does not."
~ Rupi Kaur

Yoga

My journey through yoga the past fifteen years has been one of deep self-discovery, healing, reconnecting, and ultimately life-saving. I can honestly say that I'm not sure if I would still be here today writing this book if I hadn't discovered yoga when I did. It all began when I was twenty years old, staying in my sister's cold, dark basement, drinking alcohol alone because I didn't know how to deal with the trauma I had just been through from a highly abusive relationship. Every time I would sober up an overwhelming flood of emotions and pain would wash over my being and I couldn't handle it. I didn't know how to even begin processes those dark memories and emotions, so I numbed myself. I did this for some time, maybe a year, until I realized I needed to make a living and do something with myself. I tried to go back to the gym, go hiking, meet healthy friends, attend conscious events, but I just wasn't aligning with anything.

I still went home every day and drank alone or went out and partied to distract myself from my-Self.

I have always been an active person so I knew this would somehow help me heal, but none of the activities I used to love felt good anymore. I feared that I might not ever be able to feel good again. Then I felt a calling from within, one that I could not explain but I knew I had to honor. It told me to go buy a yoga mat and start practicing every day. I did what I was told, I didn't have much to lose. Sometimes that little voice of guidance doesn't make perfect, logical sense right away but it's not supposed to. It's meant to be felt in the heart and then led by the heart, leave the rationalizing mind out of it. I didn't know much about yoga at that point. I used to compete it fitness competitions and I had attended a few classes during that time to switch up my routine. I definitely didn't know about the mental or spiritual aspects of it, as many don't in the west, I only knew about the physical benefits. And so I began practicing yoga on my little mat from Walmart in the back of my sister's yard between kid's toys and empty beer bottles. Nothing profound happened right away, but soon it became the only thing that could get me out of bed each morning. My body was gaining some of its strength back and I had energy again. Eventually I wasn't turning to a bottle for numbing, but to the mat for expansion.

One day I was attempting half-moon pose for the first time. I slowly tried to balance on one side and slipped, then hit my head hard on the shed behind me. I looked around to make sure no one saw, laughed at myself, got back up and attempted it again. I held it this time, then smoothly transitioned to the next pose and continued on with my practice. Later that day I was reminiscing on my little fall and thought, "Wow, if I could apply that mentality to my life; trying, perhaps failing, laughing and getting right back up again, what could I accomplish?" That was a defining moment in my life and the first step along the divine path of living my soul's purpose.

Years later I was living and traveling throughout Asia and decided to attend yoga teacher trainings, not because I wanted to teach but initially to go deeper into my own practice. I had already gained my physical strength back from yoga, and after my first certificate in yin yoga, I had also been emotionally healed. Yin yoga works with the energy maps (*meridians* in Chinese or *Nadis* in Indian) of the body. While most other types of yoga are *yang* and concentrate on warm, moving tissue like muscle, yin yoga stretches the cold (yin) deep connective tissue by holding poses for longer durations. Why is this important? The deep tissue is also where a lot of our unprocessed emotions are stored. An emotion is energy-in-motion, but when it isn't expressed, where does it go? It is usually repressed, held deep within, where it can later explode unexpectedly or be stored within the body potentially expressing as disease. By stretching this deep tissue we can release energy blockages and stuck emotions. I went through a whole, messy, (okay, darn right ugly) releasing, healing and rebirthing through yin yoga. I fell in love with Traditional Chinese Medicine and went on to take two more certificates in this extraordinary path of healing.

So, I had healed the physical and emotional bodies, it was time for the spiritual. Again, years later, I walked into my first kundalini women's workshop in Byron Bay, Australia. When I arrived I saw the most beautiful altar covered in colorful gems, jewels, candles and sacred items the women attending had placed down. The class was conducted by a gorgeous, voluptuous Goddess draped in white with a perfectly wrapped, large white turban. In kundalini it's encouraged to keep the eyes closed, but she was so radiant and blissful I could hardly take mine off of her the entire class! At the beginning she introduced herself and told us, "Okay ladies, it's time to take our power back!" I looked around the room nervously and thought, "Are.. Are we allowed to do that?" The other ladies seemed to think so, so I followed along. That single class was the catalyst to my deep journey of self-awakening, self-empowerment, and sexual healing. Within the year I also became certified in kundalini, but something was still missing. The final cherry on top of the many layers of cake that was my self-love journey, was Tantra. Tantra isn't what you may at first think, it's not all about sex! It's the spiritual path that embraces ALL of life and this human experience. Rather than renounce and live outside of this physical world, Tantra teaches us to embrace all of its gifts. We don't have to remain fixated on reaching higher states of consciousness through hours of practice and self-discipline. We have the capacity to reach the highest states of pure bliss and ecstasy. Right here, right now. This is why Tantra has become so sexualized, as sex is a part of life and this path doesn't discourage it, but it's not all of life. With enough practice and presence, coming together in sacred union can be just as divine of an experience as doing your laundry! As I studied ancient Tantric scripts it was like seeing everything I already knew deep within my core on paper. For me, Tantra and sacred sensuality come hand-in-hand, and with the knowledge of this path I then became a yoga teacher, but I will always remain much more a student.

As you can see from my own experience with yoga, it's not all about *asanas* and toning your booty. Actually, asana (physical poses) is only ONE step in the eight limbs of yoga by Patanjali. If you aren't familiar with the eight limbs and want to learn more about traditional yoga I suggest you begin there. Yoga is a lifestyle, capable of healing, empowering and connecting us back to our own divinity. My best advice is to be open to all types of yoga and explore to discover which works best for you. If you don't feel you are resonating with a certain practice or even a certain teacher, try something new! If I had stuck with the first type of yoga I found I would still be in short shorts at hot yoga more concerned about how I looked in a pose rather than who I could become as a person! I would have never discovered my soul purpose, became a teacher and wouldn't be writing this book now. It's important in every spiritual journey to remain open and not attach to one specific practice or teacher. Something that works for you today may not work the same for you tomorrow. While I teach Tantra now, maybe in ten years I'll be teaching something different. Allow your practices to change and grow with you. With all of the resources readily available in this technology age it's really easy to begin a yoga practice at home, or if you live in any city there's probably one around the next block! Remain with an open heart and mind and great things will come to you through the sacred art and lifestyle of yoga.

"Honour your Self. Worship your Self. Meditate on your Self. God dwells within you as you." ~ Swami Muktananda

The Chakras

"Chakras are organizational centers for the reception, assimilation and transmission of life-force energy. They are stepping stones between heaven and earth." ~Anodea Judith

Simply put, a chakra is an area of the body that is dense with energy. Chakras are the main energy centers where consciousness and matter meet, that can be visualized as different colored spinning wheels. While there are said to be many chakras throughout the body, 114 in traditional yogic belief, we can simplify it to seven main chakras that are located on the midline of the body. These begin at the base of the spine (the Root Chakra), running up to the crown of the head (the Crown Chakra), and beyond. Each chakra governs different emotional and physical aspects of the body. The lower chakras are related to our physical world and the higher chakras are related to our spiritual world, the heart is the bridge between the two. Tap into their power to live a happy, healthy and harmonious life. If you have a difficult time getting into them remember that intention is most important. Having at least a basic knowledge of the chakras can significantly deepen your healing process and journey inward.

Because each chakra is related to a different aspect of ourselves, each one impacts different areas of our wellbeing. When you learn which area associates with which aspect of your life you can then focus on balancing specific chakras to manifest certain things in your life. At perfect emotional, physical and spiritual health, the chakras are balanced, spinning effortlessly and life is beautiful. We experience a sense of fullness in all aspects. Our relationships, conversations, actions, goals, and interests flow in alignment with our highest purpose. When the chakras are unbalanced, overactive or under-active, life can be challenging. This misalignment might not be apparent on the surface, but dive deeper and you'll quickly notice where your work lays.

You can help to heal an unbalanced area by meditating on the area's corresponding colour, imagining it growing larger as a healing ball of light surrounding this region. You can also use the corresponding affirmation, oils, and crystal. Wear clothes and eat foods in the color related to the chakra. Listen to your body and tune into this area, it will tell you what it wants. It will tell you how it wants to heal.

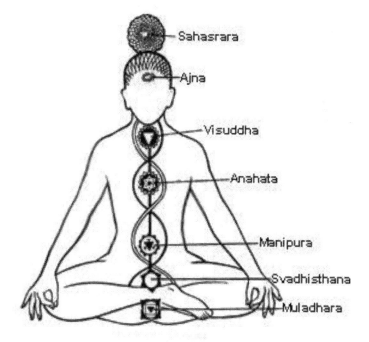

The Seven Main Chakras:

Root Chakra (Muladhara)

Location: Base of spine.

Associated with: Security, safety, shelter, grounding, support, having a foundation

Color: Red

Corresponding verb: I have, I am

When it's Balanced: Grounded, connected to earth and your family, confident, calm centered When it's weak: fear, anxiety, uncertainty, constantly living in 'survival mode', disconnection, bone/joint pain

When it's Weak: Greed, paranoia, eating disorders

Crystals: Red Carnelian, Red Jasper, Black Tourmaline, Obsidian, Bloodstone

Essential Oils: Rosewood, Rosemary, Cedar, Ginger

Affirmation: "I am strong, stable and at peace."

Sacral Chakra (Svadhisthana)

Location: Lower belly

Associated with: Emotions, sensuality, sexuality, creativity

Color: Orange

Corresponding verb: I feel

When it's Balanced: Healthy relationships and boundaries, creativity flows, shamelessly enjoys the pleasure of life through the sacred senses

When it's Weak: Dependent/Co-Dependent relationships, no control over emotions, sexual obsessions or lack of sexual desire

When it's Overactive: Overly sexual, no sense of boundaries, aggressive, arrogant

Crystals: Citrine, Orange Carnelian, Orange Calcite

Essential Oils: Ylang ylang, Clary Sage, Orange

Affirmation : "I am a sensual and sexual being. Creativity flows through me."

Solar Plexus Chakra (Manipura)

Location: Upper part of belly (where the diaphragm rests)

Associated with: Will, personal power, ego, confidence, self-discipline, independence

Color: Yellow

Corresponding verb: I can, I do

When it's Balanced: Confident, self-assured, clear focus on goals, easily manifests ideas and plans into reality

When it's Weak: Insecure, lack of clear direction or purpose, judgmental, low self-worth

When it's Overactive: Manipulative, self-obsessed, misusing personal power, ignorant, insensitive to others

Crystals: Tiger's Eye, Citrine, Yellow Tourmaline

Essential Oils: Cinnamon, Cedarwood, Ginger, Sandalwood

Affirmation: "I radiate my power into the world."

Heart Chakra (Anahata)

Location: Heart center

Associated with: Giving and receiving love, compassion, forgiveness

Color: Green

Corresponding verb: I love

When it's Balanced: Able to love and receive love openly, make decisions from the heart rather than ego, appreciation of life, deep and meaningful relationships

When it's Weak: Insecure in love, overly defensive, codependent, holding grudges

When it's Overactive: Attachment to people, being 'needy' or 'clingy', trying to please at all costs

Crystals: Pink Quartz, Clear Quartz, Jade, Green Calcite

Essential Oils: Rose, Jasmine, Ylang-Ylang

Affirmation: "I am open fully to giving and receiving love." "I forgive myself and others."

Throat chakra (Vishuddha)

Location: Throat center

Associated with: Voice, expression of truth, communication

Color: Blue

Corresponding verb: I speak

When it's Balanced: Healthy and clear expression and communication skills, honest, open, vulnerable

When it's Weak: Inability to communicate, neglect of self-care, unable to stand up for oneself, speech impairments, thyroid problems

When it's Overactive: Talk too much or inappropriately, doesn't listen to others, dishonest

Crystals: Sodalite, Turquoise, Lapiz Lazuli, Azurite

Essential Oils: Frankincense, Sandalwood, Eucalyptus

Affirmation: "I speak my truth clearly and lovingly."

Third Eye Chakra (Ajna)

Location: Third eye center, between the brows

Associated with: Vision, intuition, psychic abilities, wisdom

Color: Indigo

Corresponding verb: I see

When it's Balanced: Clear vision for oneself, clarity, good perspective on life, knowledgeable, intuitive

When it's Weak: Confusion, bad decision making, rejection of everything spiritual, headaches

When it's Overactive: Indulgence in psychic fantasies and illusions, insomnia, loss of reality

Crystals: Amethyst, Moonstone, Quartz, Purple Fluorite

Essential Oils: Marjoram, Sandalwood, Juniper, Clary Sage

Affirmation: "I see with clarity and listen to my intuition."

Crown Chakra (Sahasrara)

Location: Crown of the head and beyond

Associated with: Consciousness, higher states, bliss, liberation

Color: Violet

Corresponding verb: I know, I understand

When it's Balanced: Connected to the divine, inner peace, relaxed, aware

When it's Weak: Disconnected from Source, feeling lost, fatigue, close-mindedness, migraines, materialistic

When it's Overactive: 'Head in the clouds', disconnection from body and earth, obsessive attachment to spiritual matters, sensitivity to light and sound

Crystals: Clear quartz, Selenite, Amethyst, Charoite

Essential Oils: Angelic Root, Rose, Cypress, Lavender,

Affirmation : "I am an extension of the Divine." "I trust the Universe and am one with Universal flow."

Honoring Intuition

"Intuition is the whisper of the soul." ~ Jiddhu Krishnamurti

There's a reason it's called a woman's intuition. When you tap into your feminine power you become more sensitive to energies, including your own. This allows you to know when you are aligned with your divine path and when you are falling off of it. When you are tuned in it isn't a matter of recognizing your truth, but rather acting upon it. This is how it has been in my personal experience. All the seemingly bad or even potentially dangerous situations I have found myself in have always been after I ignored my intuition. I felt something was off, I knew it deep within, but because it didn't make 'logical' sense, my mind couldn't reason, I didn't listen to my inner guidance. There's a reason in school they tell you that your first guess is probably the correct one, then your mind begins to think of other possibilities. That feeling in your gut, that sneaking suspicion when something seems not right but you can't put your finger on why, that's your intuition. Be real with yourself and acknowledge those unsettled feelings. They are there to guide you along your highest path, listen to them. As you love yourself more you also build deeper self-trust, then doing so will become easier.

How to Recognize Your Intuition:

1. You'll feel physical symptoms such as tightness in the chest or turning in the stomach when something is "off".

2. Be honest with yourself. It's so common in today's society to push away feelings and ignore the signs. This is due to fear of change, failure, letting go, saying no, and attachment to ego. Sure, it's easier to remain comfortable and ignore the truth, but ultimately you are in control of your own happiness. If something doesn't feel right, maybe it's time for a change.

3. Pay attention to where your mind wanders. Notice if you are fantasizing about things such as quitting your job or being single, but you stop yourself, rationalizing that you wouldn't have enough money or you wouldn't be happy alone. These are your ego fears taking over from what your heart may truly want. Of course, this doesn't apply to everything, but oftentimes there is a reason our thoughts wander to certain places when we drift away from our ego.

4. Also pay attention to your dreams. If you are constantly having dreams of being in danger this may be an important message coming from within. You might have dreams of something that is off that you haven't noticed in your daily activities.

5. Watch out for synchronicity or patterns. Your intuition may be bringing certain things forth continuously in order to get your attention. Don't ignore the signs.

6. A more obvious way to recognize intuition is to speak to it directly. Meditate on the heart and ask what your intuition has to tell you, ask for divine guidance. That voice may come to you loud and clear or it may come as a soft whisper. When you have that funny feeling come up, sit with yourself and meditate on it, being open and non-judgmental to what it is trying to tell you.

Practice Gratitude

"Cultivate the habit of being grateful for every good thing that comes to you, and to give thanks continuously. And because all things have contributed to your advancement, you should include all things in your gratitude."
~ Ralph Waldo Emerson

Practicing daily gratitude is a tool that can transform your whole life. Simply changing your perspective can immediately heighten the quality of your life in every area. Even though it may seem impossible at times, during deep pain or healing from trauma we may be able to find gratitude. I started consciously bringing gratitude into my life when I'd often get stuck in a victim mentality, wondering "why me?" or be bothered by small things more than I should. When I would catch myself in those thought patterns I would replace them with thoughts of gratitude, and everything began to change! I'll admit, changing self-sabotaging thoughts for those of giving thanks isn't easy. At first this made me angry, really angry. I was in so much pain and constantly giving thanks made me feel like I was belittling my pain. I understood I should be thankful but I had other things to think and cry about! But, I stuck with it. Finally my tears stopped as this practice uplifted me every time I was tempted to go down that path of unnecessary suffering. It eventually became second nature and now I often begin listing the things I am grateful for without even realizing it. Some pain is okay, if we are learning from it, but constantly living in it for extended periods is not. I was no longer learning from it at that point but addicted to it, and practicing gratitude built my resilience and ultimately became my light out the darkness.

One recent study states that a five-minute a day gratitude journal can increase your long-term well-being by more than 10 percent! Given my personal experience, I believe it! I have been religiously keeping a gratitude journal for years, and before I even open my eyes most mornings I mentally list five things I am grateful for. Add a gratitude journal to your morning practice and write in it before you start your day, it'll change the whole vibration of the day! Another idea: For one year I wrote down what I was grateful for at the end of each day, usually things that happened and people I saw during that day, folded it up and put it in a jar. Any time I'm having a stressful day or feeling confused about existence, I go to my gratitude jar for love and inspiration!

Gratitude Meditation:

1. Lay in a comfortable position, closing the eyes and placing the hands on the heart if you'd like. Spend a few minutes tuning inward and relaxing the body.

2. Begin to think of all the events, experiences, people, pets, or possessions that you are grateful for in this life.

3. Realize, since you are reading this meditation from this book, you are already blessed with many gifts. The gift of sight, so you can see the world and acquire knowledge, the freedom of having the means to better yourself and your life however you please, the gift of heartbeat, steady, regular, and all the organs constantly working to support your life, and the gift of life itself! The most precious gift of all. Someone has birthed you, fed you, changed your diapers, gave you shelter and taught you to read and write.

The miracle that you were that one fighting sperm that made it to the egg, survived, and thrived! Our existence is truly a miracle that we should be deeply grateful for.

4. Think about all the things you have today that make your life easier and more comfortable than it was for earlier generations. Some examples:

- You flip a switch, and light appears.
- You adjust a thermostat, and a room grows warmer or cooler.
- You turn a tap and water to bathe (and possibly drink) appears
- You have a roof over your head to keep your protected and dry when rain appears and warm when winter comes. You have windows to let in natural light & see the world from the comfort of your warm home.
- You sit in front of a computer & have unlimited access to information, new connections and entertainment.
- You enter a vehicle and it takes you where you want to go.
- You have access to machines that wash your clothes for you. You have clothes previously made for your convenience.
- You have a machine that keeps your food a certain temperature all day long, and stoves to cook so you don't have to build a fire or cut wood.
- You have indoor plumbing.
- You are safe and have a system that helps you if you aren't.

5. Now, reflect on all the countless people who have worked hard, some without knowing you at all, to make your life better. Send them a thank you from your heart.

- Those who plant, grow, and harvest your food.
- Those who transport that food to markets.

- Teams of people who make roads, bridges, planes, trains & railways so you can travel.
- Teams of people who design and create the clothes you wear, the table you sit at & the bed you sleep in.
- Those who bring you your mail right to your door.
- Those who maintain the servers so you can receive and send emails and access the Internet.
- Those who gather, sort, and dispose of all your trash and recycling.
- All those who play sports, create art, music, plays, poems and films to entertain and uplift you.

6. Consider the people and animals you know who enrich your life, those who smile at you and cheer you on: family, friends, acquaintances, colleagues, and peers. Think of the beings that you have had the opportunity to connect with throughout your life. Send them all your love and gratitude.

7. Spend as much time thinking about whatever and whoever else you are grateful for. Let your heart fill with warmth and notice how your body feels after recognizing all these gifts you have been blessed with.

*"In the heart there is a brilliant lotus,
endowed with divine glory." ~ Siva Samhita*

Forgiveness

When I was traveling and learning from powerful, older women, I would often ask them if they had one gem of advice for younger generations what would it be. While I received so many beautiful snippets of wisdom, one that I heard often was that they wished they had learned to forgive earlier on in life. Holding on to grudge and pain from the past and towards others will weigh your soul down. It stays with you, and at that point you are unnecessarily suffering. In my life I have often been told that I am surprisingly good at forgiving. It's true, I have forgiven a lot, even many things that some claim to be "unforgivable". I was lucky to learn at a young age (thanks to Oprah) that everyone is doing the best they can with the life they were given, and I still do believe this.

I learned I couldn't judge anyone for their actions or feelings, and if I did I would only be hurting myself. When it became difficult to truly forgive someone, I would complete the meditation below. This came naturally to me during these times. I would do this meditation every day until I could do so without anger and tears, until I was filled with love and could genuinely wish the other person well. Sometimes this took days, sometimes months, but when you get to that place it can be one of the most liberating experiences of your life. It doesn't matter what that other person thinks, if you never receive the apology you deserve, or what they are doing now, this is about YOU and your healing journey. Remember, you come first. It's the Universe's job to worry about them, not yours. And although I would consider myself experienced at forgiving others, I found a deep challenge when it was time to learn how to forgive myself. A few years before writing this book, during my journey of self-acceptance, I had an abortion. I have lived my life in a way that I never want to look back on my death bed and say, "I intentionally hurt that person." Yes, I hurt a soul that may or may not have already existed, I terminated the possibility of life. And while this topic could be a book on its own, when all was said and done, I couldn't forgive myself. I wasn't in a place at the time to make a clear decision of whether or not I should become a mother. I couldn't forgive myself for not being stronger, for not knowing I could do it all on my own as so many women have. There was even a time I broke a hotel mirror, gashing my hand open, because I couldn't stand to look myself in the face after what I had done. It wasn't as simple as asking myself, "But what did you learn from it?" as I often do while healing from other difficult situations.

What if I told you all those difficult and dark times happened exactly how they were supposed to, in order for us to evolve? Those times are as painful as they are profound. Maybe you can't see it right away, but in time you will. Eventually, with intention and reflection, we can transform our wounds into wisdom. I am someone who personally believes that everything does happen for a reason, or at least the way it should for our own expansion. In the case of my abortion, the father was very aggressive towards me and mentally unwell. If I hadn't become pregnant and seen how unwell he truly was I may have stayed with him and put myself in a potentially dangerous situation. It took me a year after the abortion to think of the possibilities. In this realization that everything is happening in divine time and order, I eventually learned to surrender and believe that it all happened for a higher purpose. This doesn't mean that I think my actions were justified, but this helped me accept the possibilities of the situation in order to move forward.

While this topic is a sensitive one and I do still struggle with it at times, it is an example of how acceptance can lead to forgiveness and eventually back to self-love. Once I began to surrender to the situation then I slowly became more gentle and loving towards myself. Even when it's hard, overwhelming and confusing as hell, we must accept that everything we have done has made us who we are today. I do believe that the first step to self-love is accepting every part of ourselves and our unique journey. Again, we are all doing the best we can with what we have been given. That doesn't mean that everyone is trying to be good, it means we are all trying to make this mysterious and confusing thing called life work for us, based on our experiences and current level of consciousness. We can't judge anyone, even ourselves. All that we have been through was all necessary in our personal evolution to fulfill our soul's purpose in this lifetime. That situation was merely another step to get me where I am today, and that is writing this book for you. And where are you today? Reading this book and taking action to step back into that fierce, unapologetic, self-assured woman (or man) you are! That is something for us both to be proud of.

Forgiveness Meditation:

1. Find a space and time where you can be uninterrupted and give this time to yourself. If you'd like, place your favourite crystal over your heart chakra. Tune into the breath for a few minutes.

2. Recall a situation in your life that has caused you hurt or stress. Close your eyes and bring this situation to mind. Feel the struggle, distress, and emotional discomfort within your body.

3. Acknowledge that this moment hurts, is stressful, or painful. You may even speak out loud, "This hurts" or "I'm in pain." Let any emotions that come up be experienced and released.

4. Recognize that the pain, the struggle and even the suffering are all parts of life that link you to your humanity but don't have to overwhelm you. Remember that you are not alone; that all people struggle in their lives. That suffering does not mean you are less worthy, 'bad', being punished, or alone. It is simply part of this human experience. Try to embrace your pain,

it may be wanting to teach you a necessary lesson that will benefit your growth.

5. Spend a few minutes visualizing yourself as healed from each problem or person that is causing you this pain. Really picture what it'd feel like to resolve the problem or forgive the person who hurt you. How happy would you be? How would others react? How would you react to others differently? Think of all the details, really make the visualization come to life. Spend as much time here as you'd like.

6. With your eyes closed, place your hands over your heart. Take a few deep breaths and release any tension you may be holding in your body. Let all the negativity you have from these problems drain away. As you exhale, feel that stress leaving your body. Feel the gentle touch and warmth of your hands resting on your chest. Feel a warm, comforting, healing light building in your hands and spreading around your heart center. Give this healing to yourself. Allow this gentle, healing energy to flow from you and to you, spreading to your whole body and bringing calm and healing where it is needed.

7. **Forgiving yourself:** Again, visualize what life would be like if you fully forgave yourself. Ask yourself what you need to hear and feel right now to give kindness to yourself. Say to yourself, "May I be kind to myself." Speak the phrases that feel most aligned with your particular situation, such as:

- "I forgive myself."
- "I am strong and resilient."
- "I am gentle with myself."
- "I learn from my experiences, even the hard ones"
- "I accept myself as I am in this moment."
- "I give myself the kindness and compassion that I need."

- "I love myself. Every part of me, present, past and future."

8. When you're done visualizing, see these situations as if they were already resolved, just like in your visualizations. By forgiving the situation, person who wronged you, or yourself, you open up room for positive growth and abundance.

9. To conclude, you may meditate on these feelings of forgiveness or simply say "I forgive you" to each problem you listed out loud. Send the other person love. Let your emotions come up. Send all the energy you have attached to this person or situation out into the universe with love. Let the universe handle it from here, it knows what to do with it.

10. Reward yourself by taking a nice bath, getting a massage, or anything else that makes you feel like the Divine Goddess (or God) that you are!

Letting Go

The importance of practices such as yoga and meditation are to draw us inward, back to our essence, back to what is real and eternal. When we constantly look outside of ourselves we mistake everything in this physical world for being real, we want it to be everlasting. Naturally as humans we attach onto what we believe to be real whether it be material possessions, people, or our own bodies and not wanting to leave them. As we learn in Buddhism, attachment *(upadana)* is the root of all suffering *(dukkha)*. Don't be hard on yourself if this is the case, it is for most of us. Even with daily practice I still catch myself often wishing for what can't possibly last, to last. That is why consistent *sadhana*, daily practice, is so important.

More often than not our biggest challenges in life come to us when we need to learn to let go, especially in times of break ups or death. Even when these occurrences happen and we have no choice but to let go, we may still hold this individual's energy with us. This is okay if perhaps a loved one has passed and we still feel close to them. Sometimes it can become detrimental to our wellbeing when we are holding onto people who have hurt us or bring us negative energy. We may be holding onto past lovers or friends and we must let this energy go so we can make room for our own energy of pure love. I for one have always taken breakups harder than I have to, although it's gotten better I still have yet to perfect this, and maybe I never will. The following cord cutting practice has helped me a great deal to not only let go of other's energies from the past but even to let go of attachment to people in the present. You can do this meditation for people who are currently in your life as a way to stay in your own energy and not fall into negativity, attachment, and ultimately suffering.

What is cord cutting?

We create energetic cords of attachment to others we spend a significant amount of time around or form an unhealthy attachment to from afar. You can recognize this when they seem to be lingering in your mind very frequently or generally sending you less-than-desirable energy from afar. It can also be helpful when you aren't presently in a position to physically remove yourself from the person or relationship, but would like to stop the energetic drains and feelings of being deflated. Holding onto others' energies can be painful and downright exhausting. The practice of cord cutting is based on the premise that when we enter into any form of relationship with a person, an energetic thread or cord is activated. As we move through life, many relationships end and individuals move on, but these cords can still remain. And while the connection may never be fully terminated (I still have one ex-partner who I can literally "feel" entering the same room), cutting the cords can relieve us of any negative energy we may still have toward this person.

Signs You may need Cord Cutting:

- Overthinking about this person to the point you can't focus on the present
- Having repetitive conversations with them in your head
- Obsessing or seeking out ways to get revenge
- Temptation to go back to a relationship that does not serve you
- Stalker-like behaviour such as spending a lot of time on their social media or going out of your way to drive by their house
- Low energy and lack of interest in things you once loved
- Having feelings of depression and being lost

- Giving in to unhealthy habits; smoking, overeating, substance abuse
- You find yourself constantly battling illness
- Deep feelings of sadness, anger, and depression around the past

Cord cutting Meditation:

1. Sit or lay in a comfortable position and close the eyes. Tune in.

2. For this exercise we will call upon or spirit guides or angels, whichever is your personal preference. You may wish to write this out beforehand and read out loud, "I call upon (enter spirit guide, angel, etc) to help me free myself indefinitely from (insert name) so we can both move forward and enjoy our lives as whole, separate beings."

3. Imagine that you are standing on one side of a bridge, and the individual you wish to be released from is on the other side of the bridge. When you feel ready, walk towards the person and let them walk to you. Say everything you wish to say before you let them go, all the things left unsaid. Say them out loud if you'd like.

4. When you are ready, imagine a cord of dark light connecting you both at the umbilical cords, this is the energy your shared. Call upon your guides again to help you in this moment. Say, "I would now like to release and cut off any energetic ties I have to you. With forgiveness and peace, I let you go." Imagine you have a Crystal Quartz knife or scissors and cut the cord between you two. This cord releases from both of you and floats away into the universe where it will be healed and gone for good. Imagine you both now, whole on your own, with no energy shared between each other. When you are ready, go back to your side of the bridge with the intention to move forward in your life from this point on. Maybe the other person walks back to the other side of the bridge or maybe they stay in the middle because they

still feel attachment to you, that isn't your problem and will no longer effect you from here on.

5. You may notice a shift in your energy, embrace it. If you wish to stay in meditation longer, visualize yourself now moving forward in life without attachment. Imagine all the things you will now do and be freely, without that energy weighing you down.

Along with this meditation, I have found that writing a letter to the person that will never be sent (rip it up or burn it afterwards) can help a great deal in letting go of attachment, forgiving and moving on.

"Your vision will become clear only when you can look into your own heart. Who looks outside dreams; who looks inside, awakens." ~ Carl Jung

PART TWO

Embodying the Goddess

Goddess Archetypes

*"Until you make the unconscious conscious
it will direct your life and you will call it fate."* ~ *Carl Jung*

As previously mentioned, we each have the Divine Masculine and Feminine within ourselves. Because these divine energies can be difficult to comprehend from our limited human vantage, we have given them physical forms to understand better. Shakti, the feminine life energy and Creatrix of all that exists in this physical realm, has many different faces in Hinduism. These are the faces of the Divine Feminine archetypes and can also be found in many other forms in different religions and cultures. Masculine energy is also represented as Hindu Gods such as Shiva, Brahma and Vishnu. I primarily work with the Hindu deities as they resonate most with my personal path, but I have also studied and benefited from learning about Goddesses from other ancient civilizations such as the Egypt, Greece, and Ireland. In the following pages I will share my knowledge of the Hindu Goddesses and how you can apply these archetypes to your life for further personal growth.

Discovering the Goddess archetypes truly felt like that last missing puzzle piece in my journey of self-love and empowerment, which is why I have left this section for last. Once you have done the previous practices (and hopefully discovered and fallen madly in love with your-Self) it's time to go a little deeper into who you are and how you can live your best life imaginable! The many representations of Goddess lay within each of us, no matter our gender. Carl Jung, who was the first to popularize archetypes and whose work I highly recommend, explained them as "the contents of collective consciousness". They are a set of behaviours and patterns imprinted in or collective consciousness throughout time. No matter what day and age you are from, the essence of these patterns stay the same within each of us.

"In classical Tantric practice, we do this with the understanding that the goddess is not a separate entity, but an aspect of our own higher self. Invoking her unique personal presence is like tuning into a specific channel for energy and blessing, which exists in the field of the collective consciousness. Eventually, that individual form will dissolve into consciousness itself, revealing the vast spaciousness beyond forms. Along the way, as you open the borders of your psyche to the energy of the goddess, you draw her into yourself. Her qualities begin to infuse your personality, enlarge your psyche, & even create seemingly miraculous changes in outer life." ~ Sally Kempton, Awakening Shakti.

Some feminine archetypes used today that you may have heard of are the Wild Woman, the Mother, the Maiden, the Priestess, the Witch and the Creatrix. Modern patriarchy has put women mainly in the roles of Maiden and Mother, following behind is the Crone, who is now often shamed and looked down upon. It wasn't always this way. There was a time we honored and even looked up to the Crone, the old wise woman, with all of her knowledge and experience. This is shown in the way many First Nation communities treat their elders. In our society today it's become expected of us as women to be the "good girl", "strong mother" or "behaved woman". We are beyond that now. Most of us don't fit into these small boxes all of the time, we are complex multi-dimensional beings. Maybe we are the Wild Woman one day, the Hermit the next and the nurturing Mother the following day. We should no longer be limited to a couple archetypes but free to explore ourselves and be proud of all of our faces and life stages! I encourage you to explore the different approaches to archetypes and find one that most resonates with you. And while we can have all of these within us, we usually have one or two that are most dominant in our lives. Once we understand which ones we most relate to we can then learn to manage the same characteristics in our own lives. We learn how we react to certain situations and how to mold to our surroundings so we can not only be comfortable, but thrive. We can also recognize the archetype we are lacking in and learn to embrace and bring her forth. Oftentimes the Goddess we are least attracted to may actually be the one we need the most. Just like us, each archetype has a shadow Self. Once we acknowledge this shadow Self we can then become aware of when it arises, recognize when it is in excess or unbalanced and make the appropriate changes to come back to a place of balance and wellbeing.

"This meeting with oneself is, at first, the meeting with one's one shadow. The shadow is a tight passage, as narrow door, whose painful constriction no one is spared who goes down to the deep well. But one must learn to know oneself in order to know who one is."
~ Carl Jung

To give you an example of how the archetypes can help us heal I will tell you the story of me and Lakshmi. When I was a young girl I was obsessed with my looks and acquiring as much money as possible, since I grew up with very little. When I began to follow a spiritual path I shamed myself for still wanting to look beautiful or spend money on quality (even reasonable) items. I stopped wearing makeup and shaving, not because this made me feel better but because that's what I felt was expected of me in the spiritual community. I was in a constant tug-of-war between the material and spiritual world when I didn't have to be. When I discovered, and later embodied, the Hindu Goddess Lakshmi, I realized that it's possible to have a healthy relationship with beauty and materials while still remaining on a spiritual path. This was a very important realization to me as the imbalance caused me unnecessary suffering. I stopped seeing beauty and drive for success as negative things but rather just another part of my life I consciously have to keep balanced. Now when unhealthy thoughts about beauty or materials come up, I know this is Lakshmi in excess, and remind myself to come back to the balanced, graceful Lakshmi. I often do this by meditating and working with Lakshmi, as our material desires are often just a clouded desire for the Divine. Sometimes we may come out as the firey, unstoppable Kali. Before you might have again shamed yourself for your power, but when you have the awareness of Kali you can recognize her, honor her presence and remember to keep her balanced. We don't have to be ashamed of our individual complexity, again, we may be more Kali one day and more Laksmhi the next (or multiple in a day if you are a woman on her moon!) If nothing else, it sure does make this life more interesting.

In the following pages I will give an overview of the Hindu Goddesses followed by a meditation that will help you to embody and welcome each into your life. In this overview I include the corresponding chakra to each Goddess. Some systems may relate Goddesses with different chakras, this is what personally works for me. However, it's important to note that many topics in Hinduism are often open to interpretation; I may see something one way and you could see it a completely different way. That's fine! For example, when I want to embody Lakshmi, which I frequently do, I wear light purple. In my heart I feel this color represents her, as I have a painting of her beautifully decorated in lilac. The colors that usually represent her are red and gold. Even vocabulary and ancient stories can change in Hinduism depending on the region they are being told. As with many things in spiritual life, this is just a general guideline, remain open and perhaps change some small details to suit your journey best. We are ever-changing, don't take anything too seriously in this spiritual life and try not to attach yourself to one deity or belief.

Using the mantras: Mantra is a sacred tool with many personal benefits such as strengthening the mind, protecting your energy, and connecting directly to the Divine through vibration.

Repeat the following mantras 108 times for best results. In the last chapter I will explain in more detail how to use these mantras as well as some practices you can use to begin embodying the Goddess(es) of your choice.

"If there is to be a future, it will wear a crown of feminine design." ~ *Aurobindo Ghose*

Lakshmi

"Beauty awakens the soul to act." ~ *Dante Alighieri*

Lakshmi is the Goddess of wealth, fortune and prosperity. She is often called just *Sri*, which means auspiciousness. This is prosperity in all forms, not only financial but also spiritual, teaching us that we can be worldly while following a higher path. She is the embodiment of beauty, grace, harmony, and charm. Anything and everything beautiful in this world is Lakshmi. She is the feminine strength of Vishnu, one of the main Gods in Hinduism, who sustains and protects the Universe. She is most often seen in red and gold symbolizing wealth, standing on top of a lotus, with four arms. From a Tantric perspective the lotus represents reality, consciousness and karma. The lotus, which blossoms in the mud and remains clean despite its dirty surroundings, also represents purity and ability to evolve no matter one's environment. Here it is showing us that we can live in the world, just not to be possessed by the world. It's okay to embrace this material realm and all the gifts it has to offer us in this human experience (to an appropriate degree), just don't become attached or identify with these temporary luxuries.

"I am inherent in existence, I am the inciter, the potential that takes shape. I manifest myself; I occupy myself with activity, And finally I dissolve myself. I pervade all creation with vitality, will, and consciousness. Like ghee that keeps a lamp burning, I lubricate the senses of living beings with the sap of my consciousness."~ Lakshmi Tantra

Lakshmi's four arms beautifully represent *Dharma* (duty), *Artha* (material success), *Kama* (desire) and *Moksha* (liberation). In her two upper hands she holds lotuses and in the two bottom hands she holds coins falling (representing prosperity in all directions) and the other is placed in the Abhaya Mudra (representing freedom from fear). *The Bhagavad Gita* teaches that fear is caused by unfulfilled desires. The ultimate gift of this Goddess is liberating us from our fears. Some images show two elephants with upraised trunks, elephants represent life-giving rains and royal authority.

Because she is the most attractive form of Shakti, she is highly celebrated in India with temples and celebrations in her name. Lakshmi is the grace and love inside each of us and when we invoke her we go about our day with her grace beside us. The shadow Lakshmi is an obvious one that we see so often in society today; attachment to materials, compulsive consumerism, identifying with how much money one has and obsession with looking a certain way. It helps me to remember that when craving money or materials in an unhealthy manner, that this is just a craving for Lakshmi, everlasting beauty, which surpasses any temporary joy one can receive from acquiring these temporary luxuries.

Lakshmi's Profile:

Colour: Red, gold

Characteristics: Beauty, grace, love, kindness, wealth, prosperity

Consort: Lord Vishnu

Chakra: Root Chakra (*Muladhara*)

Shadow: Materialism, consumerism, greed, inequality, tainted self-image, low self-worth, attachment to anything in the physical world

Lakshmi Mantra: *Om Shreem Maha Lakshmiyei Namaha*

When to call upon Lakshmi: If you are looking for that promotion or a new beautiful home, call upon Lakshmi to bless you. If you are having self-image issues, call upon her to help you manifest a healthy relationship with your body. Invoke her for a healthy relationship with money. Ask her to remind you of what true, everlasting beauty and prosperity means.

Parvati

*"I seem to have loved you in numberless forms, numberless times,
in life after life, in age after age, forever." ~ Rabindranath Tagore*

Parvati, the daughter of the mountain, is the Goddess of sacred marriage, family and fertility. She is mother to Ganesh and the committed wife to Lord Shiva and is known for her remarkable strength, commitment and devotion (this is how she won Shiva's affection!). It is often said that to worship Shiva one must also worship Parvati, as they are One. Parvati was born to love Shiva, who at the time was committed to his own practice above all else, remaining in a meditative trance for eons. As a young woman, Parvati brought flowers and fruits to Shiva every day and decorated his cave beautifully with love and devotion. When this failed at grabbing his attention, she realized she had to match his interests and committed herself fully, and to an extreme, to her own practice. She meditated naked in harsh climates, fasted and mastered her mind to the same degree Shiva had his own. This finally won the love of the God of Destruction and they were married.

After winning Shiva's affection, she inspired him to care about the world again and then became his greatest student. It is said that Shiva had no voice until they united. As he spoke, he revealed the secrets of yoga, the Tantras and the Vedas that he had gathered during his years of meditation. These conversations between them became some of the most sacred texts in Hinduism. Parvati is the epitome of the love and devotion to one's partner. Her deep commitment to Shiva can also reflect one's own commitment to their practice and the Divine. While she is committed to her Beloved she remains committed to her own practice, as she is the yogini Goddess. She is also a relatable deity, driven by love, as so many of us are.

Parvati's Profile:

Color: Blue

Characteristics: Commitment, devotion, loyalty, family, personal will.

Consort: Lord Shiva

Chakra: Sacral (*Svadhisthana*)

Shadow: Becoming too attached to relationships and dependent on others, losing independence, becoming reliant and needy. One must remember they should feel whole on their own before beginning a relationship. Parvati and Shiva's union represents two already self-realized, powerful individuals coming together.

Parvati Mantra: *Maata Cha Paarvati Devi, Pitaa Devo Maheshvara Baandhavah Shiva Bhaktaacha, Svadesho Bhuvanatrayam*

When to call upon Parvati: She is the Goddess to turn to for help with marriage, parenting, and fertility. For strength, will-power commitment and determination in one's own practice. You can call upon her for help finding your Beloved, then after finding them, keeping the romance strong.

Durga

"Above all, be the heroine of your life, not the victim." ~ Nora Ephron

Durga (meaning *invincible* or *inaccessible*) is the Warrior Mother Goddess. The Goddess of strength, courage and justice, she is fierce like Kali but a little more composed. She is the Great Warrior Mother who helps us conquer our limitations, fears, and emotional obstacles that prevent us from shining our light out into the world. She comes in many avatars and forms in Hinduism and is worshiped as a major deity. Befitting her role as the divine guardian and protector, Durga has eight (and sometimes up to eighteen) arms, ready to battle in whichever direction needed! She holds many weapons and items such as a conch shell, bow and arrows, a lotus, a trident and a sword. These represent the strong, Queenly Goddess within each of us. She appears draped in red, completely composed and serene, on top of a tiger or lion. Like her consort Shiva, she is often referred to as the three-eyed Goddess.

While it's said that Shiva is her consort, Durga is almost always shown alone on her fierce feline. She isn't submissive to any masculine deity and she stands strong in her own power. I worked with Durga a lot when taking back my personal power and learning to stand tall on my own after years of toxic relationships. She stands outside the regular (so-called) civilized order and for one to reach her they must do the same. This includes having the courage to step away from societal expectations and the bondage of delusion and attachment.

The warrior Goddesses remind us that we have the power within to slay anything that is no longer serving our highest purpose in this lifetime. They help us destroy illusions of this physical plane and allow us to step into our personal sovereignty. It is said that Durga's protecting energy is always there waiting for you to call her in. She reminds us that we can be strong yet tender, victorious yet graceful, successful yet humble, and vulnerable yet protected.

Durga's Profile:

Color: Red

Characteristics: Strength, sovereignty, warrior, Queen, Mother, composed, guardian, inner power

Consort: Lord Shiva

Chakra: Solar Plexus (*Manipura*)

Shadow: The warrior can become too focused on wanting to win at all costs, causing them to abandon ethics in order to succeed. She can easily become caught up in ego affairs and have an unhealthy need for control.

Durga Mantra: *Aum dum durgaye namaha*

When to call upon Durga: Durga can give us strength and insight into what is needed of us in order to face our struggles and come out on top. While she is the Mother, she doesn't baby you, she reminds you of your own sovereignty. She empowers us when we need to make changes or conquer obstacles in our lives but don't know how. She reveals to us our light when we feel stuck in darkness, then guides us into it.

Kali

"You were wild once. Don't let them tame you." ~ *Isadora Duncan*

Kali is the badass warrior within each of us. She is the one who knows why she's here, what she wants and won't let anyone stop her to get it. At first, she may be off-putting to those who don't understand her, almost naked with her tongue out, holding a severed head and skulls draped around her neck. She is the only Goddess main Goddess who is shown half-nude and black. She is *The Dark One* or *The Black One*. Scary? Maybe to some, but to others she is seen as the great Creatrix of all, the *Mother of Darkness,* the one who surpasses time and space. As the dark Mother Goddess she is the vehicle for life and death, and she has the power to destroy the world. She isn't shown on an animal or lotus, but standing with one foot on her consort, Shiva, who is the only one who can calm her during her frenzy. The story goes that she was birthed from Durga's third eye to fight off an evil demon. Once in her rage she couldn't escape it and almost destroyed the world. Shiva laid himself in front of her so she would step on him and return her to her senses during her unstoppable frenzy.

The tongue is often seen as an "Uh oh!" moment when she realizes what she has done, stepping on her own Beloved. This can symbolize that we can get so caught up in our egos or emotions that we don't notice anything else around us. Others speculate that her tongue is out because she was drinking the blood of a demon, the blood representing our uncontrolled desires, so we can be liberated and awaken. Her sword slices through ignorance, delusion, lies and ego. The severed head she's holding represents the death of ego, as heads often represent the ego mind in Hinduism. Shiva and Shakti are within each of us and they must be balanced in order to live a healthy, prosperous life. If one is too dominant it can cause us to be too *tamasic* (overly extroverted, angry, passionate) or *rajasic* (overly dull mind, lazy, depressed). The goal is to become *sattvic* (calm mind, wise, aware). As scholar David Kinsley states, "it is never Kali who tames Shiva, but Shiva who must calm Kali". A Kali woman is a wild woman who can't be tamed but can be calmed for the right man. While Parvati neutralizing and soothes Shiva, Kali actively provokes and encourages him.

Kali's Profile:

Color: Black

Characteristics: Fierce, wild, dark, powerful, unpredictable, destroyer of ego, liberator

Consort: Lord Shiva

Chakra: Solar Plexus (*Manipura*)

Shadow: The destroyer can become too attached to their own desires and use their power to trample over others' feelings to feed their ego. Kali is a perfect representation of this as she becomes so caught up in slaying the demon army that she almost destroys the world. An overactive Kali can become overly aggressive or angry easily. One who abuses or overuses their power in unmoral ways.

Kali Mantra: *Om Kring Kalikaye Namah*

When to call upon Kali: If you are having low confidence or in a situation you feel you need to speak up. Confrontation isn't always a bad thing, I spent a lot of my life avoiding it, but sometimes it's necessary in order to not be walked all over or taken advantage of. Kali will help you find the personal power to set firm boundaries in relationships and stand up appropriately for your rights. She will destroys any illusions so that all negative ways of thinking and behaving can be cleared and you can move fearlessly forward.

Radha

"Only divine love bestows the keys of knowledge." ~ *Arthur Rimbaud*

Radha is the symbol of Divine, ever-lasting and ever-longing love. She is the consort of Krishna, an avatar of Vishnu and major deity in Hinduism. Along with Parvati and Shiva, Radha and Krishna are the main relationship archetypes in Hinduism. She is most often worshiped with him by her side. Their love isn't the typical Divine love however; she is a Goddess who wasn't born as a deity but a *gopi* (cow herding girl). Krishna went about his duties while Radha remained waiting for him always. They were never married, and although they lived physically separated, they remained connected by heart and soul. Radha is the maiden archetype, the young woman longing for romance. Because of her pure, absolute love for Krishna, she gained Goddess status during the bhakti (yoga of devotion) movement in India.

She sees her love in all, Krishna is everywhere, and even though she longs for him to only be hers, she knows she must share his love with the world. This, for me, is a representation of the constant struggle we have as humans to not become attached to anything in the physical world. Krishna's physical body is not what she can have all of the time, it isn't everlasting, but his love and essence is always there for her. Her longing for him transcends into a longing for the divine that we all have within, no matter which path we choose to follow. This human desire can be transformed into desire for the Divine.

Radha is a feminine energy I resonate deeply with, as I have always been a hopeless romantic. This caused me some pain in my younger years. While traveling I met a friend who was part of the Hare Krishna (Krishna devotees) movement, at that time I knew very little about Hinduism. I expressed to him that I was in a lot of pain from a recent relationship that I had devoted too much of my time and energy into while not receiving anything in return. "I have this longing to devote myself fully to someone in a way that is always taken advantage of." I told him. The next day he took me to a Hare Krishna temple and explained that I could transcend that longing into a longing for Krishna, the Divine. This was my first step into the door of Hinduism and by refocusing that desire I no longer was hurt by physical partners, but loved by the Divine.

Radha's profile:

Color: Pink

Characteristics: Hopeless love, longing, devotion, young, romance, erotic

Consort: Lord Krishna

Chakra: Heart (*Anahata*)

Shadow: Loving and giving too much with little in return, neediness, obsession, attachment to the physical, seeking validation from others, too open of a heart and not also protecting it.

Radha Mantra: *Tapta-kanchana-gaurangi, Rahdhe vrindahvaneshwari, Vrishabhahnu-sute devi , Pranamahmi hari-priye*

When to call upon Radha: When you are hurt by a longing for unfulfilled love or desires. When you wish to add romance and playfulness to a relationship. When you want to be more vulnerable or to heal from a painful break up.

Saraswati

*"As a painter paints pictures on a wall, the intellect goes on creating
the world in the heart always." ~ Brahmananda Saraswati*

Saraswati is the Goddess of knowledge, arts, creativity, learning and teaching. Her name can be translated as "flow" and "woman". The three most sacred bodies of water in India are the Ganga, the Yamuna, and the Saraswati rivers.

"The Saraswati River flows from the highest causal heavens to the earth. It is hidden underground, invisible to human eyes. In the same way, the creative force flows invisibly through the universes, connecting the dense world of forms to the world of subtle intelligence and light." ~ Sally Kempton, Awakening Shakti

She is the naturally flowing language, creativity and movement within each of us. When all of these come through as if you are being led by divine guidance, that is Saraswati. She is depicted wearing all white on top of a white lotus, representing light and truth. She allows you to act and speak in your greatest Truth. This Goddess strengthens your power of discernment, teaching you how to differentiate from impulses coming from a lower vibration and those from your highest Self. Most of all, she allows you to acquire knowledge. Saraswati is often worshiped by students, teachers, scholars, and scientists. Many musicians and performers have also shared that they call upon her before going on stage.

She is often shown with four arms, mirroring her four-armed consort Brahma, which represent *manas* (mind), *buddhi* (intellect), *citta* (creativity) and *ahamkāra* (ego). She is called the mother of the Vedas and is the creative power of Brahma, the God of Creation. In her four hands she holds a book or script (eternal knowledge, learning), a *mala* (meditation, power of inner reflection), a water pot (the power to know the difference between right and wrong) and a musical instrument (creative arts and sciences). She embodies all that is pure, flowing and sublime in Nature.

Saraswati's Profile:

Colours: White

Characteristics: Knowledge, language, expression, arts, creativity, music, discernment

Consort: Lord Brahma

Chakra: Throat (*Vishuddha*)

Shadow: Knowledge that is dominated by ego can destroy the world, it must be used with pure intention. Too much knowledge and being caught up in the mind and intellect can cause one to become disconnect from the spirit and heart.

Saraswati Mantra: *Om Aim Saraswataye Namaha*

When to call upon saraswati: If you are an artist, teacher, student, scholar, and need divine inspiration and guidance to complete a performance or task. When you want to express yourself creatively or find your voice to speak your truth.

Dhumavati

"Even as wisdom often comes from the mouths of babes, so does it often come from the mouths of old people. The golden rule is to test everything in the light of reason and experience, no matter from where it comes."
~ Mahatma Gandhi

Dhumavati, *The Smokey One* or *The Eternal Widow,* is the Goddess of disappointment. She is noticeably different from the other radiant Goddesses; she's the smokey form of Shakti, the Shakti without Shiva. She is considered ugly and is also called Alakshmi, the one who is without radiance or Lakshmi. She represents many of the things we fear as humans; unattractiveness, old age, darkness, loneliness, and letting go. It is said that she blesses those who still see the divine mother within her, past her exterior appearance. In some ancient tantric traditions, it was actually encouraged to practice sacred exercises not with your partner but with those you found unattractive, even unlovable, in order to find the Divine within everyone. Dhumavati is associated with all things considered inauspicious and unattractive in Hinduism, such as the crow which she appears to be riding on.

Dhumavati is described as a giver of *siddhis* (supernatural powers), a rescuer from troubles, and a granter of all desires. She is the Crone, the one the modern woman may not want to invoke or even look at out of fear. Crone is a word from the old word for crown, suggesting that wisdom shines around the crown chakra like a halo. Once again it is important for us to honor each stage of life. If we are aware and accept the fact that we will all be disappointed at one point or another, it will hurt a lot less than if we ignore it until it comes and we have no choice but to accept it. I, like many women today, once feared aging and saw it as a terrible thing. I didn't want to think that it would ever happen to me. Once I began traveling the world and realized that we in the west are actually privileged to grow old, I never complained about it again. It is a luxury not all those around the world have, and if you ask people from these areas I bet they would love the opportunity to grow old and wrinkly! It's all about perspective, isn't it?

Dhumavati's Profile:

Color: Grey

Characteristics: Old, dark, gloomy, ugly, alone, depression, disappointment

Consort: Widowed

Chakra: Third Eye (*Ajna*)

Shadow: Dhumavati is technically a shadow herself, but in excess can cause one to become obsessed with not aging or becoming unattractive. They might also lose compassion for those who are old, poor, or unwell. Remember, we cannot have the light without the darkness, both are very much a part of this world.

Dhumavati Mantra: *Dhum Dhum Dhumavati Svaha*

When to call upon Dhumavati: To help with accepting old age, support with letting go, to have more love for the elderly, homeless or ill, and to lose the ego mind and see others for their truth rather than their appearance.

Chinnamasta

"There is only one dream that will always be perfect in your lifetime,
And that is the dream of self-transcendence." ~ *Sri Chinmoy*

Chinnamasta is the headless Tantric Goddess in Hinduism. As with so many symbols in Hinduism, there is much more than what at first meets the eye. Her headless appearance represents transcendence of the mind and ego. Again, this is a Goddess who demands that we find the Divine within all, even in the dark and terrifying. She is one of the most outrageous forms of divinity in Hinduism and because of her ferocious appearance she is not actively worshiped everywhere. She appears nude with disheveled hair in blood red or black coloured body. She is stepping over a couple, said to be Rati, Goddess of sexual desire, and her husband Kama, God of love. She is often considered a symbol of self-control over sexual desires. She wears a serpent and a garland of skulls or severed heads similar to Kali, representing destruction of the ego. She represents three forms of transformation; life, death and sex, reminding us that we do not have to be stuck in any.

There are many ways to perceive this goddess and it all depends on your background and stage in life. Someone who is in a great deal of pain might see her image as hopeful, that it's possible to transcend suffering. Some, of course, may see her as terrifying, that might be someone who is afraid of their own demons. I for one, coming from a Tantric perspective, usually think of kundalini and the transformation of sexual energy into something greater when I look at her. Whichever way you interpret it, it's a difficult picture to ignore, and I believe that's the point. As with Dhumavati, they teach us that we can't ignore the darkness or the ugliness, but we can honor and transcend it.

Chinnamasta's Profile:

Colours: Blood Red

Characteristics: Mindlessness, egoless, transcendence, enlightenment, ferocious, sexuality

Consort: Lord Shiva

Chakra: Crown (*Sahasrara*)

Shadow: Acting mindlessly, being too concentrated on reaching higher states that one misses the beauty in the present moment. Losing foundation and connection to earth.

Chinnamasta Mantra: *Srim hrim klim aim Vajravairocaniye hum hum phat svaha.*

When to call upon Chinnamasta: When you are too caught up in your ego and need to transcend it. When you need assistance seeing a situation from a higher perspective in order to heal or move on from it. For spiritual guidance. For hope out of a dark period in your life.

Goddess Embodiment

Now that you have an understanding of the archetypes, some of the main Hindu deities and how they apply to your life, and maybe even figured out which one you most resonate with, it's time to fully embody the Divine Feminine. You can use these practices with any form of archetype you would like. Although in Hinduism, there are three main ways to embody and worship the Goddesses. These are through the use of mantra, yantra, and physical images.

Mantra:

"What is a mantra? Mantra is two words: Man and tra. Man means mind. Tra means the heat of life. Ra means sun. So, mantra is a powerful combination of words which, if recited, takes the vibratory effect of each of your molecules into the Infinity of the Cosmos. That is called 'Mantra.'" ~Yogi Bhajan

Mantra are the spoken (or thought of) vibrations of the Divine. In Tantra, mantra is the most powerful way to worship the Goddesses. This is because it is speaking the vibration of Shakti, and the universe is said to begin with a single vibration. By speaking and singing these mantras you are getting on to the same vibration of the Goddess and awakening her within. From vibration you are making manifest the Divine. There are mantras for many frequencies other than the Goddesses, such as the chakra mantras. The most known mantra is the *Om (or Aum)* mantra, which is said to be the sound of Brahman, the primordial sound of creation. It is recommended to chant each of the mantras 108 times each day, this is a very significant number in Hinduism. While I gave one mantra for each Goddess, I encourage you to do your own research and find one that you'd like to work with, as there are many mantras for each Goddess. It's also a good idea to learn some sanskrit pronunciation, you can find videos online or buy a book, I personally took mantra classes and they helped a great deal. Most Hindu mala beads, garlands, or prayer beads, come with 108 beads for chanting. Simply place your fingers over each one as you go until you reach the big starter bead. If you are having difficulty with some of the mantras, simply chant "Maaaaaa", this is the universal sound of Mother.

Yantra:

"Yantra meditation helps us clear the content of our consciousness so it can become a pure mirror, reflecting without interpreting. All That Is exists infinitely in this emptiness, this no-thing-ness. When the mirror of our consciousness is left without any content, this is enlightenment." ~ Ivan Rados

Yantra are geometrical shapes that represent the energy field of the specific deity. Yantra is the form while mantra is the energy or consciousness. A common one you may have seen around is the Sri Yantra, which is a 12,000-year-old diagram commonly called the mother of all yantras. This diagram is said to represent the all existence; the cosmos and the human body. Place a Yantra on your wall or have it on your altar, meditate on its meaning and image for deeper concentration or use it in ceremony.

Images:

"Only the images we live can bring transformation." ~ Helen Luke

Of course, images are also a great way to worship and embody the Goddesses. By giving them physical form we can have a greater understanding for what they represent as well as relate easier. My first experience of non-duality (being One with the Divine) was through meditating on a photo of Durga. I didn't know this belief system existed and didn't know much about the Goddesses at the time either. I had just listened to my intuition and kept a framed picture of her in the back of my van I called home. I have never felt such a complete Oneness with a deity as deeply since that experience. I felt her awakening inside of me, and I knew then that we were both faces of the same energy. Keep a picture of the Goddess(es) you are working with on your altar and around the house. Make offerings to her, complete puja, meditate, sing mantras and speak to her beautiful image.

Goddess Embodiment Puja:

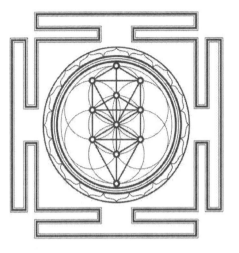

This is a practice you can use to welcome one or multiple goddesses into your life and to fully embody each. When I first used this meditation I practiced for one month straight and was never the same again- I was an awakened, self-realized, multifaceted GODDESS! In my morning practice I worship and embody three to four goddesses I am deeply resonating with at the time, welcoming each into their corresponding chakra. The following is an example of my practice, but using all seven Goddesses. Of course, you can change the Goddesses to whichever and however many you would like.

1. Sit comfortably in front of your altar or somewhere where you have Goddess Yantra or images present. If this isn't possible, imagine you are in front of these representations of Shakti. I often bring offerings like flowers or light a candle for Mother.

2. I begin my puja by chanting the mantra for Shakti: Om Shakti Om, either 108 times or a dozen times if I am short on time. Chanting the full 108 times allows you to transcend form, and moving back to the yantra and images brings you back to form. While chanting Shakti, my hands are on my heart, her home.

3. I then place my hands facing downward to the earth and the base of my spine, meditating on the root chakra and welcoming in Lakshmi. While Saraswati represents the earth element, I always feel Lakshmi in my root chakra because she represents everything you need to create a good foundation to build your life upon. Again, this is open to interpretation and you can use either. I will repeat the Lakshmi mantra three times, meditate on her image or yantra, close my eyes and breathe in her energy. I then visualize myself embodying Lakshmi, radiating all of her best qualities; beauty, kindness, love and prosperity.

4. I bring my hands to my sacral chakra, welcoming in Parvati. Again, some feel this is Lakshmi's corresponding chakra but I feel parvati represents love, boundaries and healthy relationships, all resonating with the sacral area. Again, I chant, welcome her, and visualize myself as her.

5. Next, bringing my hands to the solar plexus chakra, I do the same with Kali or Durga. This is the region of your personal will and power.

6. Bringing both hands over my heart, I repeat with Radha and often also Krishna, the great Divine lovers.

7. Bringing my hands to the center of my throat, I repeat the same with Saraswati. Often asking her to guide me to communicate my highest truth and express my divinity through creative form.

8. Next, I bring my focus to my third eye chakra, usually with my hands in prayer pose at this region, and repeat with Dhumavati. As I visualize myself embodying her, I am reminded that this physical form is only temporary and not to become too attached to it. I am reminded that beauty and wisdom comes in all forms.

9. Finally, I open my hands above the crown of my head and repeat with Chinnamaster. Rather than actually visualizing myself with no head, I visualize myself with great commitment to my practice, the Divine, and transcending the ego.

10. When I'm done I will thank each of the Goddesses and go about my day with this experience in mind, applying all of these energies to my life.

"Rise Goddess, rise and meet this day. Child of the earth and the stars, the heartbeat of the universe is within you. So breathe. Breathe and let the winds of your spirit guide. Relieve your shoulders of the burdens. You are meant to fly."
~ S.C Laurie

Thank you for reading!

If you enjoyed this book or found it useful along your journey, I'd be very grateful if you'd post a short review on Amazon. Your support really does make a difference and I read all the reviews personally so I can get your feedback and make this book even better.

Your support is deeply appreciated!

- Krystal Aranyani